UNFAILING

UNLIKELY PEOPLE

DARK
HORSE

MATT

CHAPPELL

First published in 2016 by Striving Together Publications, a ministry of Lancaster Baptist Church, Lancaster, CA 93535. Striving Together Publications is committed to providing tried, trusted, and proven books that will further equip local churches to carry out the Great Commission. Your comments and suggestions are valued.

Striving Together Publications
4020 E. Lancaster Blvd.
Lancaster, CA 93535
800.201.7748

Cover design by Andrew Jones
Layout by Craig Parker
Edited by Lesley Gonzalez

The author and publication team have put forth every effort to give proper credit to quotes and thoughts that are not original with the author. It is not our intent to claim originality with any quote or thought that could not readily be tied to an original source.

ISBN 978-1-59894-328-3

Printed in the United States of America

DEDICATION

This book is dedicated to two men who have made an incredible investment in my life and whose examples I have been proud to follow. First, to my dad, Dr. Paul Chappell: thank you for your love, constant guidance, and godly leadership of our family. Thank you for your heart for developing young leaders and the invaluable lessons you've taught me with your own life about excellence in ministry.

Second, I dedicate this book to my uncle, Pastor Steve Chappell: thank you for being a godly mentor, helper, and role model over the last several years that I have been blessed to serve alongside you. Your vision to empower young leaders is inspiring. Thank you for your wisdom, encouragement, support, and your prayers as we prepare for the next phase of ministry.

+ +

CONTENTS

+ +

Introduction vii

1. Who Would've Thought 1

2. Stop the Water 21

3. Trash Talk 47

4. The Struggle is Real 67

5. Hook in the Nose 89

6. The Heart of a Dark Horse 107

Conclusion 127

Notes 131

INTRODUCTION

Do you remember having friendly (or not-so-friendly) sword drill competitions when you were growing up? If you've spent most of your life in church as I have, you're no stranger to this old time Sunday School or youth group favorite, but in case you're new to it, I'll explain. You sit among a group of other kids, each of you holding your Bibles high in the air in one hand (the spine goes flat against your palm—no cheating!) and you wait for your group leader or another adult to call out random Scripture references. After repeating the reference to be sure everyone understands, the leader calls out *Go!* and the first person to find and read the correct passage wins.

I'll let you in on a little secret: I was pretty much a sword drill ninja back in my day. I loved that game. There's nothing quite like the rush of whizzing through those pages and speed scanning passages to find just the right verse and elbowing your neighbors or shouting over the kid in the back (who probably had his whole Bible tabbed and indexed anyway) so you can be the first to claim victory—oh, is that not how you play? Inevitably during the game, the group leader would yell out a reference like Hezekiah 1:7, and I'd start searching all over the place. One problem: there is no book of Hezekiah. I fell for it every single time.

Actually, because of sword drills, for years the only thing I knew about Hezekiah was that he was definitely not a book in the Bible. I knew all about David and Solomon and other larger-than-life kings whose stories are recorded in God's Word—but who was Hezekiah? Even today, many people you ask can't tell you who Hezekiah was or what he did. And the first time I typed *Hezekiah* on my computer, I got that weird little squiggly red line because not even my software recognized his name!

As it turns out, Hezekiah was pretty awesome. He was the king of Judah responsible for ridding the nation of idols and reestablishing worship at the temple, bringing spiritual reform to the people. It's of King Hezekiah that the Bible speaks in this verse in 2 Kings:

He trusted in the LORD God of Israel; so that after him was none like him among all the kings of Judah, nor any that were before him.—2 KINGS 18:5

Basically, the Bible says that Hezekiah was one of a kind—in the good way. Now *that* is high praise. Yet, when Hezekiah was young and even when he first became king, I doubt many people could have predicted God would use him to do phenomenal things. In fact, based on his background Hezekiah was a pretty unlikely candidate for greatness. But if there's one thing I hope you learn from this study, it's that God uses unlikely candidates to demonstrate His unfailing power. He's not concerned about our ability; He's looking for our availability.

> He's not concerned about our ability; He's looking for our availability.

Hezekiah can teach all of us a thing or two about what it means to trust God and be used by Him to do what we could never accomplish on our own. Throughout the chapters of this book, I hope you will be inspired by Hezekiah and use your life to do great things for God.

1

+ +

WHO WOULD'VE THOUGHT

+ +

2 Kings 18:1–8

The date was November 6, 1860, and a bitterly divided nation headed to the polls to determine its next leader. The Republican candidate for president was a former one-term congressman who was still a relative political unknown despite failed attempts to win a seat in the U.S. Senate; in fact, his name didn't even appear on the ballot in nine states.[1] Nonetheless, against three other contenders and with 40 percent of the popular vote, by the end of the day Abraham Lincoln had been declared the sixteenth President of the United States, and he would go on to become one of the most well-known and well-loved leaders in all of American history.

Nearly one hundred years later, in November of 1950, 30,000 United Nations troops under the leadership of Major General Oliver Smith of the U.S. Marine Corps found themselves completely surrounded by 120,000 Chinese troops in the Chosin Reservoir of North Korea. Certain of victory, the Chinese forces launched a series of attacks intended to completely annihilate the UN troops, but they were met with a surprising resistance. Refusing to go down without a fight, over the next weeks the UN troops (later nicknamed "the Chosin Few") made a strategic retreat from the area while inflicting so many casualties on the Chinese Army that China's technical "victory" in forcing the UN out of Korea was hollow, essentially viewed as a defeat.[2]

Finally, on a chilly afternoon in February of 1980, a seventh-seeded U.S. hockey team captained by a then-unknown Mike Eruzione faced off against a much more experienced, multi-gold medal winning Soviet "dream team" in the Lake Placid Winter Olympics, having just been soundly beaten by the same team in an exhibition game days before. By the third period of intense play, the score was tied 3–3 when a powerful shot by Eruzione gave the U.S. the lead for the first time in the game. The underdog American team managed to hold onto the lead for ten more brutal minutes until the final horn sounded a victory that was so surprising it became known as the "Miracle on Ice," one of the greatest upsets in sports history.[3]

What do these three incredible stories have in common? Each one tells of a somewhat unknown or unlikely candidate who comes from behind to unexpectedly succeed. While we might call this type of person an *underdog*, Merriam-Webster's dictionary gives a more intriguing name: *dark horse.*

One thing I love about the Bible is that it's filled with dark horse stories. David was an unknown shepherd boy who went on to defeat an older and much more experienced warrior (not to mention giant!) who had long terrorized Israel (1 Samuel 17). A farmer named Gideon, an unlikely choice for an army general, led 300 men in battle against a 135,000-man enemy army—and won (Judges 7–8). And what about Esther? The Jewish orphan living as a captive in Babylon who was suddenly elevated from obscurity to national fame when she married King Ahasuerus—and then went on to save all the Jews in the kingdom from extinction at the hands of Haman (Esther 4–5).

With all these and more miraculous stories, we can only conclude that our God loves to demonstrate His power and bring victory through the most unlikely "dark horse" candidates. And Hezekiah was no different. Although by the end of his life he would be known as one of the greatest kings of the Bible, no one would've guessed that by how he began. But as we'll see, despite the obstacles to greatness in Hezekiah's path, he chose to trust God and do right, and as a result he was blessed far beyond anything he—or anyone else—could've imagined.

THE OBSTACLES HE FACED

The first verses of 2 Kings 18 introduce us to Hezekiah and let us know the timing of his becoming king of Judah:

> *Now it came to pass in the third year of Hoshea son of Elah king of Israel, that Hezekiah the son of Ahaz king of Judah began to reign. Twenty and five years old was he when he began to reign; and he reigned twenty and nine years in Jerusalem. His mother's name also was Abi, the daughter of Zachariah.*—2 KINGS 18:1–2

Obstacle #1: His Culture

The Bible includes the detail that Hezekiah became king *"in the third year of Hoshea son of Elah king of Israel."* A brief look to other passages shows us what else was going on during this time. Second Chronicles tells us that Judah was in pretty bad shape:

> *For the Lord brought Judah low because of Ahaz king of Israel; for he made Judah naked, and transgressed sore against the Lord.*—2 CHRONICLES 28:19

Hezekiah ascended to the throne at a dark time in his nation's history. As a punishment from God for the wickedness of Hezekiah's father, Ahaz, Judah had been attacked by its enemies and many of its people had been taken captive. What's worse, the people that were left in Judah were not praying for God's mercy.

Thanks to Ahaz, the temple of God had been closed, and instead, altars had been built in *"every several city of Judah"* for the people to worship false gods and engage in all sorts of other wicked acts (2 Chronicles 28:24–25).

If you think Hezekiah's situation of being surrounded by a corrupt culture was unique to him, take a look around you. A survey by the Pew Research Center released in 2015 found the percentage of the U.S. population identifying themselves as Christian has dropped significantly since 2007, while the percentage of the population identifying themselves as "atheist, agnostic, or nothing in particular" has risen.[4] Meanwhile, crime and wickedness abound, making more and more Americans afraid for the future and for the safety and wellbeing of their families. In late 2015 Chapman University released its "Survey of American Fears," which listed Americans' top fears as government corruption, corporate corruption, cyber terrorism, and terrorist attacks.[5] Just like Hezekiah, we live in a time of confusion and corruption, but the Bible warned us this was to be expected:

> *This know also, that in the last days perilous times shall come. For men shall be lovers of their own selves, covetous, boasters, proud, blasphemers, disobedient to parents, unthankful, unholy, Without natural affection, trucebreakers, false accusers, incontinent, fierce, despisers of those that are good, Traitors, heady, highminded, lovers*

of pleasures more than lovers of God; Having a form of
godliness, but denying the power thereof: from such turn
away.—2 TIMOTHY 3:1–5

Obstacle #2: His Father

Have you ever been embarrassed of your parents? With a dad like
Ahaz, Hezekiah must certainly have been reluctant at times to
admit whose son he was. All our passage tells us is Ahaz's name,
but earlier in 2 Kings we read this:

> *In the seventeenth year of Pekah the son of Remaliah Ahaz*
> *the son of Jotham king of Judah began to reign. Twenty*
> *years old was Ahaz when he began to reign, and reigned*
> *sixteen years in Jerusalem, and did not that which was*
> *right in the sight of the LORD his God, like David his*
> *father. But he walked in the way of the kings of Israel, yea,*
> *and made his son to pass through the fire, according to*
> *the abominations of the heathen, whom the Lord cast out*
> *from before the children of Israel. And he sacrificed and*
> *burnt incense in the high places, and on the hills, and*
> *under every green tree.*—2 KINGS 16:1–4

Ahaz wasn't just an embarrassment; he was a selfish man and a
wicked king. He disobeyed God's commands, actively participated
in idol worship, and led his people to join him, going so far as to
destroy the vessels of worship in the temple and close down the

temple so no one could worship there (2 Chronicles 28:24). But if you skimmed over those verses, go back and at least read verse 3. Did you see what makes Ahaz pretty much the worst dad ever? That verse tells us that Ahaz ritually sacrificed his own children to pagan gods. He was killing his own kids in some act of false worship! In fact, some suggest the only reason Hezekiah did not die like his siblings before and after him was because his mother saved his life.[6] Can you imagine?

In comparison to Ahaz, I bet your parents don't seem as embarrassing anymore! If you were raised by parents or a family who loved and protected you, and above that, who loved God and taught you to love and obey Him, I hope you realize how blessed you are and how thankful you ought to be. I hope you repay their goodness to you by honoring them as the Bible teaches:

Children, obey your parents in the Lord: for this is right. Honour thy father and mother; (which is the first commandment with promise;) That it may be well with thee, and thou mayest live long on the earth.—
Ephesians 6:1–3

But maybe like Hezekiah you came from a difficult family background. Maybe your parents weren't Christians or maybe they were never there for you like parents should be. One thing I want you to take from this chapter is that Hezekiah didn't let his family past determine his future. He realized that he still had the power to choose whether or not he would obey God for himself. You too should realize that although your earthly family situation may be difficult, you have a heavenly Father who loves you more than you could ever dream and wants to use you in a great way just like Hezekiah.

Obstacle #3: His Youth

Did you know that there's an age requirement to be President of the United States? To even qualify to lead our country, you have to be at least thirty-five years old. Well, Hezekiah couldn't have been president here, because he was only twenty five (2 Kings 18:2). Young rulers were not all that uncommon in those days; in fact, Hezekiah's father was closer to twenty years old when he began to reign.[7] And of course we know there were even younger kings, like Josiah, who was just eight years old when he was crowned (2 Kings 22:1). But while Hezekiah wasn't the youngest king around, he certainly could have used his age as an excuse and could have believed he was too young to do anything significant for God.

> Too many young people use their age as an excuse not to get serious about God.

Too many young people use their age as an excuse not to get serious about God. They think they have all the time in the world to live for God later as soon as they're done having a little "fun" first. This is a dangerous attitude. None of us know how long we have to live, and terrible things can happen when young people decide to live for the present and grow up later. Instead, we should be passionate for God now while we can. That was Charles Spurgeon's attitude. He preached his first sermon at age sixteen, just a few days after he was baptized, and by age seventeen, he was already pastoring a church.[8]

You are never too young to start living for God.

> *Let no man despise thy youth; but be thou an example of the believers, in word, in conversation, in charity, in spirit, in faith, in purity.*—1 TIMOTHY 4:12

> *Then said I, Ah, Lord GOD! behold, I cannot speak: for I am a child. But the LORD said unto me, Say not, I am a child: for thou shalt go to all that I shall send thee, and whatsoever I command thee thou shalt speak.*—JEREMIAH 1:6–7

THE OPPORTUNITY HE TOOK

We've seen that Hezekiah faced some pretty big obstacles to greatness when he first took the job of being Judah's king. And considering where he had come from, how young he was, and how depressing the times were, it would've been much easier for Hezekiah to just throw up his hands and decide there was nothing he could do to make a difference. It would've been easier to just follow in the footsteps of his wicked father and let his people continue sinning against God. But maybe Hezekiah realized that obstacles often pave the way for greater opportunity. You see, God knows how to take a setback and use it as a setup for His glory. And as Hezekiah considered his kingdom and his responsibility as Judah's leader, he saw opportunities to do the right thing and to succeed where his father had failed. Thus, we read in 2 Chronicles and 2 Kings that Hezekiah's reign was completely opposite his father's from the very beginning:

> *And he did that which was right in the sight of the* LORD, *according to all that David his father had done. He in the first year of his reign, in the first month, opened the doors of the house of the* LORD, *and repaired them. And he brought in the priests and the Levites, and gathered them together into the east street, And said unto them, Hear me, ye Levites, sanctify now yourselves, and sanctify the house of the* LORD *God of your fathers, and carry forth the filthiness out of the holy place.*—2 CHRONICLES 29:2–5

> *He removed the high places, and brake the images, and cut down the groves, and brake in pieces the brasen serpent that Moses had made: for unto those days the children of Israel did burn incense to it: and he called it Nehushtan. He trusted in the* LORD *God of Israel; so that after him was none like him among all the kings of Judah, nor any that*

were before him. For he clave to the LORD, and departed not from following him, but kept his commandments, which the Lord commanded Moses. And the Lord was with him; and he prospered whithersoever he went forth: and he rebelled against the king of Assyria, and served him not. He smote the Philistines, even unto Gaza, and the borders thereof, from the tower of the watchmen to the fenced city.—2 KINGS 18:4–8

Let's look at three specific opportunities of which Hezekiah took advantage.

Opportunity #1: Restoring Focus on God

A 1933 radio address by then-president Franklin D. Roosevelt introduced the concept of using "the first one hundred days" of a first-term presidency to measure a president's accomplishments because the first days are when a new president's influence is greatest.[9] Since then, politicians and pundits have often debated how a president's first one hundred days in office can establish a president's legacy and predict the direction of the country over the next four years.

If those politicians had been around for Hezekiah's first one hundred days, they would've been shocked at how quickly he got to work making some much-needed changes around Judah. Second Chronicles 29 tells us that one of the very first things Hezekiah did after becoming king—in fact, in the very first month of his reign—was restore the temple in order to turn the people away from their idol worship to worship the only true God.

In your life, what you fixate on becomes your focus. When I was a senior in high school, I really wanted a car. Not just any car, I wanted a 2002 black BMW. At the time, that was the coolest car in my opinion, and I was constantly looking online to try to find one for sale. I was on Craigslist and Auto Trader daily looking for a 2002 black BMW. For the next few weeks whenever I was around town you know what car I kept seeing everywhere? Yep, a 2002 black BMW. The truth is there were no more 2002 black BMWs on the road than there had been before I started searching. But what you fixate on becomes your focus.

When we put our eyes on Jesus and He becomes our focus, we'll start to see His evidence all around us. His evidence was always there but now we have a renewed focus on Him. Maybe today instead of focusing on our situation, we should focus on our Saviour.

> In your life, what you fixate on becomes your focus.

This determined focus on turning back to God would establish Hezekiah's legacy as a reformation king throughout history, but I doubt he was worried about his legacy at that time. Instead, Hezekiah was worried about pleasing God and trusting Him to turn the hearts of the people toward Himself once again. Hezekiah commanded the priests and Levites to cleanse themselves of sin first, then to rid the temple of the wicked idols and filth that had filled it during Ahaz's reign. The rest of 2 Chronicles 29 describes how the priests and Levites took days to clean the temple completely and restore the vessels of worship that Ahaz had desecrated. The people then made offerings of atonement to the Lord to signify their readiness to worship and obey Him once more.

If we are to overcome obstacles that have been set before us and to do great things with our lives, we must make sure our focus is in the right place.

Hezekiah's cleansing of the temple showed he trusted in God and not in himself to get Judah back on track.

Opportunity #2: Removing the Idols

After cleansing the temple and restoring the nation's focus on God, Hezekiah's next opportunity was to destroy the false idols and places of worship that had distracted the people for so long. Judah had been steeped in idolatry and immorality thanks to the wickedness and disobedience of Ahaz. In fact, 2 Kings 18:4 shows us that the people had even gone so far as to take the bronze serpent, the symbol of God's redemption from sin during Moses' time (Numbers 21), and had begun worshipping it and burning incense before it. And when the verse speaks of the "groves" that Hezekiah cut down, the word in Hebrew refers to places built to worship Asherah, the Canaanite goddess of fertility, with rituals and practices of sexual immorality (2 Kings 16:4).

Hezekiah could have just considered his job done with the reopening and cleansing of the temple, but he knew those idols and groves had no place among people that were supposed to be trusting in God. He was not going to leave it to chance that the people would continue to focus on God and not return to their wicked ways—these things had to be removed completely. What in your life needs to be removed in order for you to be renewed?

I once heard a Haitian pastor illustrate to his congregation the need for total commitment to Christ by telling a story of a man who wanted to sell his house for $2,000. Another man wanted very badly to buy it, but because he was poor he could not pay full price. After much bargaining, the owner agreed to sell the house for half the original price under one condition: he would retain ownership of one small nail protruding from just over the front door.

After several years, the original owner wanted the house back, but found the new owner was unwilling to sell, so he went out and found the carcass of a dead dog and hung it from the single nail he still owned over the front door. Before long, the entire house became unlivable and the family was forced to sell the house to the owner of the nail. All the second owner had to do was remove the nail over the door and the whole issue could've been avoided. Thus, the Haitian pastor concluded, "If we leave the devil with even one small peg in our life, he will return to hang his rotting garbage on it, making it unfit for Christ's habitation."

How true that statement is! We cannot be fully committed to God while we hang onto even the tiniest habit or reminder of sin. We may not think that small sin is a big deal, but Ephesians 4:27 says we aren't to leave even the smallest foothold for Satan to grab onto in our lives because even small sins can lead

> What in your life needs to be removed in order for you to be renewed?

to big destruction. Instead, Hebrews 12 instructs us to "...*lay aside every weight, and the sin which doth so easily beset us*" so that we can fully focus on what truly matters.

Opportunity #3: Rebelling against Wickedness

Although Hezekiah had restored the temple and rid the land of idols, he wasn't done yet. Second Kings 18:7 tells us the third opportunity he saw to get his nation back on track:

> *And the Lord was with him; and he prospered whithersoever he went forth: and he rebelled against the king of Assyria, and served him not.*—2 KINGS 18:7

When we hear the word *rebellion*, we typically think of someone who is refusing to follow authority in order to go his own way or to do something bad. But in this case, rebellion was a good thing. The king of Assyria was someone Ahaz had partnered with in the past. He had made a deal to pay tribute to the king of Assyria in exchange for protection from the Philistines and other enemies who were attacking Judah. But if you recall anything about the history of the Israelites, you'll remember that Assyria was a wicked nation and an enemy of God, and Ahaz had no business making any deals with them.

Sometimes you'll hear people justify compromising themselves or their beliefs by saying something like, "It's for the greater good" or "It's the lesser of two evils." Remember in Daniel 6 where the princes and presidents tried to take Daniel out by having the king make a decree that no one was to pray to any god but the king or risk being put to death in the lions' den? What if Daniel had thought, "Well, it's either pray to the king or be put to death. Praying to the king is the lesser of two evils…and after all, it's just for thirty days"? I wonder how that story might have ended differently if Daniel had compromised his faith in that way? But we don't have to wonder, because Daniel knew that compromise wasn't an option. He rebelled against the wicked law, and by his actions he essentially said, "It doesn't matter what they do to me; I'm going to keep praying to God."

In the same way, although refusing the king of Assyria meant losing protection against attacks from other enemies, Hezekiah refused to compromise. He rebelled against the wicked Assyrian king and refused to honor the deal Ahaz had made with him. With his actions, he was essentially saying, "You don't control us anymore. We belong to God, and we're going to follow Him."

THE OUTCOME HE EXPERIENCED

So far, Hezekiah's reign has been characterized by some bold moves and big risks. He's tossed out the idols, cleaned up the temple, and thrown off an oppressive "partnership" with the Assyrians that threatened to leave Judah unprotected against its enemies. How did these moves, which were based entirely on his trust in God, pay off?

They paid off big time.

> And the Lord was with him; and he prospered whithersoever he went forth: and he rebelled against the king of Assyria, and served him not. He smote the Philistines, even unto Gaza, and the borders thereof, from the tower of the watchmen to the fenced city.—2 KINGS 18:7–8

Strength

We see in verse 7 above that as a result of his obedience to the Lord, Hezekiah "prospered whithersoever he went forth." And 2 Chronicles gives us an even more detailed picture:

> And Hezekiah had exceeding much riches and honour: and he made himself treasuries for silver, and for gold, and for precious stones, and for spices, and for shields, and for all manner of pleasant jewels;—2 CHRONICLES 32:27

God blessed and provided for Hezekiah and strengthened the entire kingdom through Hezekiah. What a turnaround from the dark days that Judah had seen under Ahaz! When we serve God faithfully, He will supply our needs generously.

Success

God wasn't done blessing Hezekiah. Not only did God take care of Hezekiah's material needs, but He also took care of Judah's enemies. Second Kings 7:8 tells us that Hezekiah defeated the Philistines. Remember, the Philistines were the enemy that had been dominating the nation since Ahaz's time. Ahaz had tried to defeat them, but where he failed because of his wickedness, Hezekiah succeeded because of his obedience.

Remember, there's a direct connection in our lives between obedience to God and the spiritual success we experience. God taught this principle to Joshua, another great leader of His people, as Joshua set out to replace Moses:

> *This book of the law shall not depart out of thy mouth; but thou shalt meditate therein day and night, that thou mayest observe to do according to all that is written therein: for then thou shalt make thy way prosperous, and then thou shalt have good success.*—JOSHUA 1:8

Before February 15, 2006, few people outside of Greece, New York, knew the name *Jason McElwain*. (If you don't know it, look it up on YouTube right now. It's awesome.) A high-functioning autistic athlete, Jason was serving as the manager of Greece Athena High School's basketball team under Coach Jim Johnson when he got the chance of a lifetime. Close to the end of the last quarter of a game in which Greece Athena was dominating its rival for the division title, Coach Johnson decided to put Jason in the game. Jason missed his first two shots, but in the four minutes of play that followed, he sank six three-pointers and a two-pointer for a total of twenty points. Not only did Jason tie the school's three-point record, but he made national headlines.

What a great dark horse story! No one could've predicted Jason would succeed the way he did. Coach Johnson put him in the game, and it unlocked his potential. In the same way, Hezekiah's success couldn't have been predicted either. He was the son of a wicked man who had a history of killing his own children, and he was heir to the throne of a small nation with big troubles. But God prospered him and unlocked his potential.

God wants to unlock your potential, too. He wants you to experience His unfailing power in such an incredible way that people will look at your life and ask, just like with Hezekiah, "Who would've thought?"

2

+ +

STOP THE WATER

+ +

2 Chronicles 32:1–8

Have you ever wished you could have a do-over in life? Think about the last bonehead mistake you made—the big test you failed because you didn't take the time to study or the good friendship you messed up because you were selfish or mean. How great would it have been to just hit a rewind button and get a second chance to fix those mistakes?

Not too long ago, I made a mistake that had the potential to impact my family in a big way. My wife, Katie, is a firm believer that real Christmas trees are the only way to go. Every year I try to convince her to side with me and get a fake tree because there are so many benefits: they last forever, which makes them cheaper in the long run, they're easy to unpack and pack, they're much less messy, they look perfect every time...I could go on. But every year she says, "No," and so every year, we drive to a Christmas tree lot to pick out a tree.

To me, the process of picking out a Christmas tree is simple. You look around for a minute or two until you see one that's cheap and isn't lopsided or missing a huge section of branches at the back, and then you pay for it and get back home as quickly as possible, mission accomplished. How great does that sound? Well, to Katie, it didn't sound great at all. So a couple of years ago when I rushed us into the lot expecting to find a tree in the first five minutes of being there, she wasn't too happy with me. I wasn't super engaged in the whole process of figuring out which tree was just "perfect" for us, and the lines were so long and the lot was so crowded that I got frustrated, and we ended up leaving with no Christmas tree at all. A few hours later, after we'd had some time to relax, we headed back to the lot, and after an hour we had picked a tree. But I hadn't brought any twine or rope to tie it to our Jeep, and the lot owners only gave us a bit of twine that wasn't nearly strong enough to secure the tree. We ended up driving home with both of us tired and frustrated, our arms stretched out the windows trying to keep the tree from flying off the roof.

I learned that for Christmas Katie and I had completely different philosophies about tree shopping. I thought picking a tree was about being fast and efficient, but to Katie, it's all about the experience. She explained how important it was to her to make the experience fun and memorable by playing Christmas music in the car on our way to the lot, stopping by Starbucks for coffee, taking family selfies, and really taking our time to pick out a great tree. I hadn't done any of those things. I'd really messed up.

Thankfully, last Christmas I got a do-over, and you better believe I took advantage of it. We took our time. We laughed together. I played Katie's favorite Christmas tunes in the car. I even brought some rope to tie down the tree (Turns out 250 feet is a bit excessive). I was prepared! And on our way to the lot, I started to turn in to a Starbucks. At first Katie pretended this part of the experience wasn't a big deal. She said, "That's okay, we don't really need it." But alarm bells in my head warned me this was a trap, so I pulled into the drive-thru anyway. Afterward, we took our time picking the perfect tree and singing together with the kids on the ride home. We did the whole experience. And guess what? Katie was right; it was pretty fun.

I'm so glad we serve a God of second chances and do-overs. He knows we make mistakes, and because of His grace, He gives us new beginnings and new opportunities.

> It is of the Lord's mercies that we are not consumed, because his compassions fail not. They are new every morning: great is thy faithfulness.—LAMENTATIONS 3:22–23

Therefore if any man be in Christ, he is a new creature: old things are passed away; behold, all things are become new.—2 CORINTHIANS 5:17

In Chapter 1 we saw how Hezekiah had a great start to his reign in Judah, restoring the temple, destroying the idols and high places, and defeating the Philistine army that was trying to control the land. But Hezekiah also knew what it meant to make a mistake that needed a do-over.

In 2 Chronicles 32 we are introduced to a new king of Assyria, a man named Sennacherib (try saying that five times fast!) who comes on the scene after Hezekiah had been king for about fourteen years. Remember how in Chapter 1 Hezekiah rebelled against Assyria and refused to pay the tribute his father Ahaz had agreed to pay Assyria for protection? Well, Sennacherib didn't like the new arrangement, so he retaliated with a sneak attack that destroyed the *"fenced cities"* (surrounding cities) of Judah, and Hezekiah was blindsided. He wasn't ready. But Hezekiah's mistake wasn't in not being able to predict that Assyria would attack Judah; his mistake was in how he handled it. Instead of trusting God, he trusted in himself and responded in the wrong way.

Life has a way of throwing us all a curve every once in a while. Everything will be going great, and then all of a sudden, your dad will lose his job or a loved one will have an accident or a serious health problem. You can't always control what happens to you. But you can control your response to what happens to you. And one of the first steps in responding the right way is recognizing that challenges and difficulties will come your way and knowing where you need to turn and in whom you need to trust.

That's why the Bible tells us to get ready for spiritual warfare. We need to know that battles and difficulties are coming so we can prepare our response ahead of time.

> *Thou therefore, my son, be strong in the grace that is in Christ Jesus. And the things that thou hast heard of me among many witnesses, the same commit thou to faithful men, who shall be able to teach others also. Thou therefore endure hardness, as a good soldier of Jesus Christ. No man that warreth entangleth himself with the affairs of this life; that he may please him who hath chosen him to be a soldier.*—2 TIMOTHY 2:1–4

But here's where God's new mercies come into the picture. Although Hezekiah's initial response was not one to be proud of, the Lord allowed him to begin again and get back on track. And there are four lessons we can learn from his example that will help us have our response ready the next time we get blindsided by a challenge and need a do-over.

LESSON #1: DON'T ALLOW FEAR
TO ELIMINATE YOUR FIGHT

To understand the context of what's happening in 2 Chronicles 32, we can turn back to 2 Kings 18, which happens at the same time chronologically. Verse 13 of that chapter tells us this:

> *Now in the fourteenth year of king Hezekiah did Sennacherib king of Assyria come up against all the fenced cities of Judah, and took them.*—2 KINGS 18:13

In case you're wondering where this Sennacherib guy came from, you should probably know that he was no stranger to fighting against God's people. His dad Shalmaneser, the previous king of Assyria, had waged war against the nation of Israel earlier in Hezekiah's reign and taken the Israelites captive (verse 11). Now his son was making trouble for Judah, all because Hezekiah had refused to pay tribute to Assyria any longer.

Assyria was a powerful and dangerous enemy, and when Sennacherib destroyed the fenced cities of Judah, Hezekiah got nervous—and probably more than a little scared. But instead of responding in faith, he responded in fear.

Charles Earl Boles (also known as Charles E. Bolton) earned a place in history as the legendary outlaw and stagecoach robber Black Bart. Between 1875 and 1883 he robbed twenty-one stagecoaches, stealing tens of thousands of dollars worth of cash and valuables from Wells Fargo and passengers unlucky enough to be traveling the western frontier unprotected. But Black Bart never once fired a weapon in any of his robberies. In fact, many times he didn't even use a real gun. His weapon was intimidation through fear. He hid his face with a hood, and his sinister presence was enough to paralyze his victims.[1]

> Satan tries to use the power of fear to paralyze your progress for God.

In the same way, Satan tries to use the power of fear to paralyze your progress for God. He doesn't want you to succeed in life, so he employs one of his greatest tactics to hold you back or to force you to respond in the wrong way. Look what problems fear caused for Hezekiah.

Fear Caused Confusion

Read what happened in 2 Kings 18:14:

> *And Hezekiah king of Judah sent to the king of Assyria to Lachish, saying, I have offended; return from me: that which thou puttest on me will I bear. And the king of Assyria appointed unto Hezekiah king of Judah three hundred talents of silver and thirty talents of gold.*
> —2 KINGS 18:14

Did you see that? That was Hezekiah telling Sennacherib, "I have sinned against you." All he'd done was refuse to be subject to a wicked nation that was the enemy of God. He hadn't sinned, but his fear made him second-guess his decision to rebel against Assyria in the first place. His fear made him think, "Maybe that wasn't such a good idea after all. Maybe I should have just paid the tribute like my father." His fear made him apologize for the very thing he'd done right.

When you're living by fear instead of by faith, you can get confused just like Hezekiah because that's what fear does. It clouds your vision and makes you second-guess yourself. Fear is the reason you question your decision to invite a neighbor to church and suddenly start thinking about how awkward things will be between you or imagining he or she thinks you're weird now. Fear is the reason you begin to wonder if you made a mistake about getting involved in church ministries or activities, and you tell yourself you really don't have much time so it was probably a bad idea. Fear is the reason you start to doubt that you should've given so much in the last Christmas offering because you don't see God blessing your finances in the way you hoped he would.

> But we have to remember that God is a God of second chances, not second guesses.

You see how the devil has a way of getting us to doubt our right decisions? When what we experience is different from what we expected, we can sometimes doubt what God has called us to do. But we have to remember that God is a God of second chances, not second guesses. If He puts something on your heart to do, you must do it. Don't let fear hold you back. Instead, let faith lead the way, knowing that God is not the author of confusion (1 Corinthians 14:33), and He will never set you up to fail.

> *Fear thou not; for I am with thee: be not dismayed; for I am thy God: I will strengthen thee; yea, I will help thee; yea, I will uphold thee with the right hand of my righteousness.*—ISAIAH 41:10

> *Nay, in all these things we are more than conquerors through him that loved us.*—ROMANS 8:37

Fear Caused Compromise

Merriam-Webster defines *compromise* as "a way of reaching agreement in which each person or group gives up something that was wanted in order to end an argument or dispute."[2] Essentially, to compromise is to give in or to make a deal. And that's what Hezekiah did with the king of Assyria: he gave in and made a deal. He compromised his convictions.

> *And Hezekiah king of Judah sent to the king of Assyria to Lachish, saying, I have offended; return from me: that which thou puttest on me will I bear. And the king of Assyria appointed unto Hezekiah king of Judah three hundred talents of silver and thirty talents of gold. And Hezekiah gave him all the silver that was found in the house of the Lord, and in the treasures of the king's house.*

*At that time did Hezekiah cut off the gold from the doors
of the temple of the Lord, and from the pillars which
Hezekiah king of Judah had overlaid, and gave it to the
king of Assyria.*—2 KINGS 18:14–18

Hezekiah promised to pay whatever price Sennacherib
wanted, and that price (verse 14) ended up being high; in our day,
it would've been about $1.4 million. That's a lot of money! But
what's worse than the decision to pay the enemy is where Hezekiah
got the money: he stole it from the temple of God.

There's no way that Hezekiah could have known when all this
trouble began that he would end up robbing the temple to meet
Assyria's demands. But that's how sin works. It takes you further
than you ever wanted to go, and you end up doing things you never
thought you would do. Satan will do anything in his power to get
you to compromise your spiritual convictions, and that's why you
have to determine, before the challenges ever come, that there are
certain things you won't budge on, ever.

Have you ever seen "House Hunters"? It's basically a show for
anyone who likes to watch other people buy new houses. It's pretty
fun. One of the common questions you'll hear a real estate agent
ask someone on the show looking for a new home is "What are
your non-negotiables?" Essentially they're asking, "What have you
pre-determined that you must have, no matter what? What have
you *pre-determined* that you will not accept, no matter what?"

I think that's a good question when it comes to compromise in our lives that might sidetrack our progress or testimony for God. What are your spiritual non-negotiables? What actions—like tithing, church attendance, or getting in God's Word daily—have you pre-determined to do faithfully, no matter what? What actions or attitudes have you pre-determined have no place in your life, no matter what?

> What are your spiritual non-negotiables?

One thing you have to remember if you're going to refuse to allow fear to compromise your convictions and eliminate your fight is that we can always rely on the strength of the Lord:

> *I sought the Lord, and he heard me, and delivered me from all my fears.*—PSALM 34:4

If we are going to change the world, we've got to be confident in Christ, not cowering in concern.

LESSON #2: RECOGNIZE THE ENEMY DOES NOT FIGHT FAIR

In 1896, the world welterweight boxing champion was a man named Norman Selby, professionally known as "Kid McCoy" (from which we get the term "the real McCoy"). In addition to his "corkscrew punch," McCoy was known for many things, but what made him popular in the ring, ironically, was his cheating and underhanded tactics. He considered nothing beneath him in order to win, including spraying ammonia in his opponents' eyes or scattering thumbtacks under their bare feet. In one fight, McCoy learned his opponent was deaf and decided to use this to his advantage. Close to the end of the third round, he stepped back and pointed to his opponent's corner, indicating the bell had rung to end the round, although it really hadn't. When his opponent turned his head, McCoy unloaded a powerful blow that knocked him out cold.[3] Was it fair? Definitely not. But it was effective.

So far, we've seen Hezekiah cower in fear of Assyria's advancing army and compromise his convictions by stealing from the temple to pay Sennacherib in hopes that the attack would stop. In 2 Chronicles 32 Hezekiah learned his enemy was not about to fight fair.

> *And when Hezekiah saw that Sennacherib was come,*
> *and that he was purposed to fight against Jerusalem,*
> —2 CHRONICLES 32:2

See the Deception

Hezekiah's deal with Sennacherib was that if Hezekiah paid the money, Assyria would stop advancing on Judah. But after the money was paid, Sennacherib continued his attack, and this time he aimed for Jerusalem. He'd lied to Hezekiah; he never intended to keep his end of the deal! Like the cheating boxer, Sennacherib was going to do whatever it took to win.

We need to realize that Satan never fights fair. He advertises fun and pleasure, but his actual product is agony and defeat. The temptation to compromise ourselves and to sin never delivers what it promises. We shouldn't be surprised by this. The Bible tells us that Satan is a liar and a deceiver by nature:

> *Ye are of your father the devil, and the lusts of your father ye will do. He was a murderer from the beginning, and abode not in the truth, because there is no truth in him. When he speaketh a lie, he speaketh of his own: for he is a liar, and the father of it.*—JOHN 8:44

If we aren't careful, we'll listen to the enemy's lies, and that's exactly when he'll go for the knockout punch.

See the Destruction

When Hezekiah looked out to see Sennacherib advancing, he realized that Sennacherib had never wanted to help him at all; he wanted to hurt him. He saw the Assyrian king's ultimate goal was not to negotiate for more money or more control over Judah. He intended to destroy both Hezekiah and Jerusalem.

Sometimes the way we talk or make jokes about Satan makes it seem that we don't believe he's really as evil as the Bible says he is. We must understand Satan is not just out to trick us into doing bad things every once in a while. He is a dangerous enemy who is on a warpath to destroy us.

> *Be sober, be vigilant; because your adversary the devil, as a roaring lion, walketh about, seeking whom he may devour:*—1 PETER 5:8

> *The thief cometh not, but for to steal, and to kill, and to destroy: I am come that they might have life, and that they might have it more abundantly.*—JOHN 10:10

The enemy the Bible speaks of doesn't want to negotiate or pick a little fight with us. He wants an all-out war. Satan wants to use our mistakes to cripple us, but God wants to use our mistakes to cultivate us. So when you find yourself in the middle of an attack from an enemy who doesn't fight fair, recognize that you have a place to turn:

> *What time I am afraid, I will trust in thee. In God I will praise his word, in God I have put my trust; I will not fear what flesh can do unto me.*—PSALM 56:3–4

LESSON #3: ANTICIPATE THE ATTACK

In the moment that Hezekiah saw the deception and destruction of Sennacherib, he was like the prodigal son who *"came to himself"* (Luke 15:17) and saw things clearly for the first time. He realized his fear had only led him and the nation into deeper trouble. Hezekiah needed to make things right—so he prepared for battle.

I played basketball throughout high school and college, and I remember one particular occasion when my team played an opponent that just wiped the court with us. After the game, our coach told us one of the major reasons we lost was that we didn't run an effective press break against the other team's defense. So our team got to work. We ran press breaks relentlessly, over and over again at every practice, until we improved. And guess what? The next time we played that team, we were prepared. We could anticipate their attack, and we had an answer ready for them.

> Satan wants to use our mistakes to cripple us, but God wants to use our mistakes to cultivate us.

When we are attacked spiritually, we need to do the same thing. We need to recognize where we've gone wrong and take action. But how do we do that? How do we make sure we are prepared? Let's look to Hezekiah's example.

Stop the Water

Read what happens next in 2 Chronicles 32:

> *He took counsel with his princes and his mighty men to stop the waters of the fountains which were without the city: and they did help him. So there was gathered much people together, who stopped all the fountains, and the brook that ran through the midst of the land, saying, Why*

should the kings of Assyria come, and find much water?
—2 Chronicles 32:3–4

Hezekiah realized Jerusalem's water supply was running beyond the city walls into the outer cities and supplying the Assyrian armies encamped there. He knew if Judah was going to win the war, they couldn't afford to give the enemy such an advantage. So he called his advisors to help him stop the water supply.

If we are going to win the spiritual battles we face on a daily basis, we can't give our enemy any unnecessary advantages. See how the apostle Paul put it:

> *To whom ye forgive any thing, I forgive also: for if I forgave any thing, to whom I forgave it, for your sakes forgave I it in the person of Christ; Lest Satan should get an advantage of us: for we are not ignorant of his devices.*
> —2 Corinthians 2:10–11

Like Hezekiah, many times we also supply "water" that gives our enemy an advantage over us. We flirt with the enemy. We don't distance ourselves from ungodly influences. We continue to go to places we know aren't good for us. But in the Bible we are told:

> *But put ye on the Lord Jesus Christ, and make not provision for the flesh, to fulfil the lusts thereof.*—Romans 13:14

For he that soweth to his flesh shall of the flesh reap corruption; but he that soweth to the Spirit shall of the Spirit reap life everlasting.—GALATIANS 6:8

If you want to win the war, stop the water. Don't sow to the flesh. Don't give it an advantage over you. Stop the water.

Not too long ago, Katie and I made a decision to invest in our home and put in some grass. If you've ever been around new grass, you know you have to take care of it and give it lots of water, especially in the beginning. The only problem was that before long, we started seeing notices around our neighborhood and from the water company that because our state was in a drought, we needed to conserve water by not using it on the grass. We had to stop the water. You can guess what happened: after just a few days without water, our beautiful grass withered up and died. Without water, it couldn't grow.

> If you want to win the war, stop the water.

Spiritually speaking, without the supply of "water" to our flesh, the sinful desires of our hearts can't grow either. So be smart: determine to stop the water by distancing yourself from bad influences. Don't even go near places or people you know will bring nothing but temptation.

A prudent man foreseeth the evil, and hideth himself: but the simple pass on, and are punished.—PROVERBS 22:3

Strengthen the Walls

Hezekiah's next move was to make sure the city was protected against Assyria's attacks:

> *Also he strengthened himself, and built up all the wall that was broken, and raised it up to the towers, and another wall without, and repaired Millo in the city of David, and made darts and shields in abundance.*
> —2 Chronicles 32:5

The battle was coming. Hezekiah knew that if Jerusalem was going to withstand an attack, its defenses needed to be strengthened. The broken wall was the city's weak point; if Sennacherib could get through it, the entire city would be vulnerable. So Hezekiah got to work rebuilding the walls.

In the same way, if we are going to withstand spiritual attack, we need to identify the weak points where the enemy will most certainly attack us and get to work rebuilding some walls. What area of your life needs rebuilding? Is it your devotional life? Your time with your family? Your commitment to volunteer with a church ministry? Your health? Or maybe you don't need to rebuild a wall; maybe you need to build a wall that's never been in your life before. Maybe you need to start some healthy physical or spiritual habits that will strengthen you. Whatever it is, determine what areas in your life need work and take action.

What area of your life needs rebuilding?

Supply the Weapons

After attending to the walls, Hezekiah took inventory of the weapons that were available to his army (verse 5). He knew that winning a war requires a good supply of offensive and defensive weapons. The same is true spiritually.

(For the weapons of our warfare are not carnal, but mighty through God to the pulling down of strong holds;)
—2 Corinthians 10:4

But what are our spiritual weapons?

Put on the whole armour of God, that ye may be able to stand against the wiles of the devil. For we wrestle not against flesh and blood, but against principalities, against powers, against the rulers of the darkness of this world, against spiritual wickedness in high places. Wherefore take unto you the whole armour of God, that ye may be able to withstand in the evil day, and having done all, to stand. Stand therefore, having your loins girt about with truth, and having on the breastplate of righteousness; And your feet shod with the preparation of the gospel of peace; Above all, taking the shield of faith, wherewith ye shall be able to quench all the fiery darts of the wicked. And take the helmet of salvation, and the sword of the Spirit, which is the word of God:—Ephesians 6:11–17

Ephesians 6:17 tells us the Word of God is our weapon to stand against the enemy. We know it's the most effective weapon because Jesus used it when He was tempted in the wilderness (Matthew 4). If the Word of God was how Jesus defended himself against Satan, how much more so should we turn to it in our daily spiritual battles?

LESSON #4: SPEAK LIFE TO THOSE AROUND YOU

Hezekiah has come quite a long way since those first verses of 2 Chronicles 32. Instead of trusting in God, he let his fear of the Assyrians influence him into making a pretty big mistake. But then he realized his enemy's true motives and determined to make things right. Now he's preparing for war, which is what he should've done in the first place.

> Once you decide to do what's right, the next step is to involve those around you.

In Hezekiah's preparations we see another lesson: once you decide to do what's right, the next step is to involve those around you. As king of Judah, Hezekiah had a great responsibility to lead his people, and he understood that if Jerusalem was going to withstand Assyria's attack, it would take all of their working together. So he gave a powerful speech meant to encourage and inspire them.

> *And he set captains of war over the people, and gathered
> them together to him in the street of the gate of the city,
> and spake comfortably to them, saying, Be strong and
> courageous, be not afraid nor dismayed for the king of
> Assyria, nor for all the multitude that is with him: for
> there be more with us than with him: With him is an arm
> of flesh; but with us is the Lord our God to help us, and to
> fight our battles. And the people rested themselves upon the
> words of Hezekiah king of Judah.—2 CHRONICLES 32:6–8*

By now you've probably heard it so many times it seems cliché: our words have power. We can impact other people's attitudes and actions just by the words we use. We can make someone's day with a nice compliment or ruin someone else's self esteem with one careless or mean remark. James put it this way:

> *Behold also the ships, which though they be so great, and
> are driven of fierce winds, yet are they turned about with
> a very small helm, whithersoever the governor listeth.
> Even so the tongue is a little member, and boasteth great
> things. Behold, how great a matter a little fire kindleth!*
> —JAMES 3:4–5

Speak Encouragement

The Bible says that Hezekiah *"spake comfortably"* to the people (verse 6). He knew the people were as scared as he'd been himself not too long before, and they needed to be encouraged. The word *encourage* means to give confidence or hope—quite literally, it means to *put courage in* someone.[4] These people needed courage put into them, and as their leader, Hezekiah was the one to do it.

We all need others in our lives to help us be courageous at times. Even the author of one of the most inspiring speeches in American history, Dr. Martin Luther King, Jr., needed encouragement. The original speech he intended to give at the March on Washington did not have the words "I have a dream" in it. But as Dr. King neared the conclusion of his speech, he found he was having trouble closing it in a way that felt "just right." He needed something to give his audience that would inspire them in a way that nothing had before—but he didn't know quite what to say. Then, from off to one side, his friend the famous gospel singer Mahalia Jackson shouted, "Tell them about the dream, Martin!" From this encouragement history was made.[5]

There is power in words of encouragement. Who in your life have you encouraged lately?

Speak Edification

As Hezekiah spoke "comfortably" to the people, he reminded them of some important facts: they were not alone in the war, the Lord was on their side, and He would fight for them. Hezekiah's words helped *edify* the people, or helped build them up and increase their confidence. We can use our words either as bricks to build others up or as bullets to tear them down. The choice is up to us, but we have a clear direction from the Bible:

> *Wherefore comfort yourselves together, and edify one another, even as also ye do.*—1 THESSALONIANS 5:11

See the Effect

At the end of verse 8 we see how Hezekiah's encouragement impacted the people:

> *And the people rested themselves upon the words of Hezekiah king of Judah.*—2 CHRONICLES 32:8

Do you remember the feeling when you were a kid of being soothed and comforted whenever your parents told you "Everything's going to be okay"? You immediately felt better about whatever situation you were facing because you trusted your parents, and you knew you could believe them. This is the same idea we get from the words *"rested themselves"* in verse 8. The people found comfort and hope in the things Hezekiah told them because they knew they could believe him.

Hezekiah knew his people were going to need significant encouragement if they were ever going to move forward and win the battle, so he determined to speak life to them. I want to encourage you to do the same for others in your life.

Thomas Edison is remembered as the greatest inventor of all time. He invented the microphone, the phonograph, the incandescent lightbulb, talking movies, and more than one thousand other things. One invention that consumed a lot of his time was the storage battery. He worked on it for more than ten years and intended to use it in automobiles.

In December of 1914 the film room of his plant erupted into flames from a spontaneous combustion of chemicals, and within minutes, all Edison's materials and supplies, including his storage battery prototype, had gone up in flames. Fire engines from eight surrounding towns arrived to help with the blaze, but the heat was so intense and the water pressure so low that their help was futile. Everything was destroyed.

The sixty-seven-year old Edison watched calmly as his possessions burned, knowing there was nothing he could do. After the fire was doused, Edison thoroughly surveyed the damage and estimated his loss at over $900,000—a huge figure that would be roughly $23 million in today's dollars. His plant's insurance would only cover about one-third of the total damage. Still, as Edison surveyed the ruins, he said, "There is great value in disaster. All of our mistakes are burned up. Thank God we can start anew."[6] Weeks later, Edison secured a loan from Henry Ford to get his

> But, just remember God can take your mess and turn it into a message.

plant up and running again, and he and his team went on to make almost $10 million in revenue the next year.

The prophet Isaiah wrote,

Remember ye not the former things, neither consider the things of old. Behold, I will do a new thing; now it shall spring forth; shall ye not know it? I will even make a way in the wilderness, and rivers in the desert.—ISAIAH 43:18–19

No true dark horse story comes without failure. Sometimes we can just plain make a mess of things, but just remember God can take your mess and turn it into a message. Hezekiah took advantage of his second chance to respond to the enemy's attack, and this time, he did it the right way. Today, I hope you're thankful for a God who allows us a second chance to fix our mistakes and begin again.

3

+ +

TRASH TALK

+ +

2 Kings 18:17–37

Have you ever been intimidated by the way someone spoke to you? Or on the flip side, have you ever been the one intimidating others by how you talk? I wouldn't consider myself someone who is easily intimidated, but sometimes people can say certain things or say things in a particular way that just gets under your skin. For me, one of those times was when I was playing basketball in college. I don't even remember what team we were playing or whether we were winning, but I clearly remember being out on the court and hearing someone from the stands shout, "Hey 21!" (that was my number) "I didn't know Barbies played basketball!" At first I wanted to laugh. Let's be honest, that's kind of funny. But the more I thought about it, the more that comment got in my head. I found myself scanning the stands, trying to figure out who had yelled out. Later, I realized that even though I'd thought the comment hadn't bothered me, it had done exactly what whoever yelled it intended—it threw me off focus just enough so that I wasn't playing my best.

Michael Jordan is widely considered one of the greatest players in the history of basketball. (Personally, I'm a Kobe fan, but I guess Jordan was *okay*.) With six NBA championships, five regular season MVP awards, three all-star MVP awards, and an Olympic gold medal, Jordan was certainly one of the most decorated players in the league. But aside from his athletic ability, one thing Jordan was famous for was his ability to get into his opponents' heads with intimidating trash talk on the court. During one faceoff between the Orlando Magic, Jordan dominated top Magic scorer Nick Anderson by telling Anderson his moves beforehand: "I'm coming down. I'm going to dribble it between my legs twice. I'm going to pump fake and then I'm going to shoot a jumper. And then I'm going to look at you." Jordan followed through and delivered that final look, and Anderson could only stare back helplessly.

Jordan's trash talk has been credited for throwing his opponents off their game and even for ruining their careers. In the 1995 NBA Playoffs as the Charlotte Hornets were trailing the Bulls by one point, Muggsy Bogues took possession of the ball with Jordan guarding him. After a while Jordan—who was over 6 feet tall—stopped guarding and stepped back to give the 5′3″ Bogues space to shoot, delivering a pointed insult about Bogues' height. Bogues later said that moment ruined his career, and it certainly seemed to be true, as his average points per game were cut by half for the rest of his time in the league.

Trash talking is almost expected in sports, and while between friends it can just be a way of joking and having fun, one of the uses of trash talk in competitive situations is to shake opponents' confidence and make them fear or even believe they'll be defeated. In 2 Kings 18, the people of Judah find themselves in a situation where their confidence is being attacked. While Sennacherib had certainly tried to do that a short time earlier with his deception, this attack was different because it was entirely a war of words.

In Chapter 2 we discovered that Hezekiah came back from a pretty big mistake and prepared himself and his people for Assyria's attack against Jerusalem. In 2 Kings 18, as they waited for the enemy to attack, they were approached by some of Sennacherib's messengers, led by a man named Rabshakeh. (These names just keep getting weirder, don't they?) Rabshakeh set himself up in a place where all of Jerusalem could see and hear him. Instead of offering news of peace or further compromise, he strategically and skillfully mocked the people and began to intimidate them.

> *And Rabshakeh said unto them, Speak ye now to Hezekiah, Thus saith the great king, the king of Assyria, What confidence is this wherein thou trustest?* —2 KINGS 18:19

Rabshakeh delivered a stinging speech with the goal of making the people afraid. This is an interesting contrast to Hezekiah's last speech to them, which was intended to give them courage. Now, instead of feeling powerful, the people felt panic. Could they believe what Hezekiah had said about God giving them the victory over Assyria? Or were they going to believe the words of the enemy standing before them with his massive army to back him up?

We've been talking in this book about dark horses, unlikely candidates who come up from a place of obscurity or disadvantage to claim victory. I'll tell you right now, no dark horse ever experienced victory by listening to an enemy's trash talk. But I'll also tell you, there will be times in your life when you feel like trash talk is all you can hear around you. Times when your faith is tested and you're bombarded with lies and feelings of discouragement, fear, insecurity, and condemnation. How do you combat the lies these voices tell you that are meant to shake your confidence and test your faith in God?

Right voices lead to right choices.

The first step is to determine which voices you're going to listen to. Right voices lead to right choices. You must recognize that the voice of the enemy will only speak lies meant to break you down and make you doubt yourself and your God. If you listen to this voice, it will steer your life into the path of destruction. So don't listen! Don't believe the voices that say you're not good enough. Instead, learn to hear and focus on the voice of truth which comes from God's Word and from people He places in your life to guide you in the right direction. Let's look to Rabshakeh's speech to find five common lies the enemy voices will tell us and five truths straight from God's Word we should listen to instead.

LIE #1: YOUR PAST WILL HAUNT YOU FOREVER

Rabshakeh's first move is to attack Hezekiah's past mistakes. We know Hezekiah wasn't perfect. In fact, that's what makes him such a great dark horse. He didn't have it all together. Just a few verses before this, he stole money from the house of God to pay Assyria. Now thanks to Rabshakeh we learn another mistake he made:

> And Rabshakeh said unto them, Speak ye now to Hezekiah, Thus saith the great king, the king of Assyria, What confidence is this wherein thou trustest? Thou sayest, (but they are but vain words,) I have counsel and strength for the war. Now on whom dost thou trust, that thou rebellest against me? Now, behold, thou trustest upon the staff of this bruised reed, even upon Egypt, on which if a man lean, it will go into his hand, and pierce it: so is Pharaoh king of Egypt unto all that trust on him.—2 KINGS 18:19–21

Hezekiah had made an alliance with Egypt, yet another wicked nation Judah had no business dealing with. You remember Egypt, right? As in the same place where God's people were enslaved for four hundred years and the place where God brought all those plagues to punish Pharaoh for refusing to let the people go? What was Hezekiah thinking trusting Egypt again?

> *Woe to them that go down to Egypt for help; and stay on*
> *horses, and trust in chariots, because they are many; and*
> *in horsemen, because they are very strong; but they look*
> *not unto the Holy One of Israel, neither seek the Lord!*
> —Isaiah 31:1

Rabshakeh asked the same question, but his point was to mock the deal because at that time, Egypt was not a strong nation and would be an undependable ally. In fact, he called Egypt a "bruised reed," or a weak stick that wouldn't be able to support Judah but would break if they leaned on it for support.

Probably the worst part about Rabshakeh's words is that they were absolutely right. Hezekiah had made yet another big mistake that could put his people at risk. But where Rabshakeh was wrong was in implying that Hezekiah's mistake was permanent, that it would break and hurt him so much that he could never recover.

TRUTH #1: YOUR PAST DOESN'T DEFINE YOU

The enemy wants you to believe your mistakes are who you are, and that you can never get past them. This lie brings thoughts of guilt and condemnation that can tear you down and feelings of insecurity that stop right in its tracks whatever progress you're making in life. But here's the truth: God can take your mistakes and turn them into miracles. Here's the truth: when Jesus died on the cross to bring your forgiveness of sins, that forgiveness was unconditional. When you trusted Him as your Saviour, He made you a completely new creation.

> *Therefore if any man be in Christ, he is a new creature: old things are passed away; behold, all things are become new.*—2 CORINTHIANS 5:17

God can take your mistakes and turn them into miracles.

The truth is, in Jesus, there is no reminder of the mistakes you made in your past. There is only grace and forgiveness, love and rest.

> *As far as the east is from the west, so far hath he removed our transgressions from us.*—PSALM 103:12

So when Satan tries to remind you of your past, silence that voice by reminding him of his future:

> *And the devil that deceived them was cast into the lake of fire and brimstone, where the beast and the false prophet are, and shall be tormented day and night for ever and ever.*—REVELATION 20:10

LIE #2: YOU ARE POWERLESS

After Rabshakeh reminds Hezekiah of his mistakes, he turns his taunting on the people of Judah:

> *Now therefore, I pray thee, give pledges to my lord the king of Assyria, and I will deliver thee two thousand horses, if thou be able on thy part to set riders upon them. How then wilt thou turn away the face of one captain of the least of my master's servants, and put thy trust on Egypt for chariots and for horsemen?*—2 Kings 18:23–24

He told the people that even if the king of Assyria straight up *gave* them horses for the fight, they probably didn't have enough trained riders to even make use of them. Burn! At that point, some of Hezekiah's men stepped in. They could see the impact Rabshakeh's words were having on the people, and they tried to slow him down by asking him to speak in the Syrian language, which they could understand but the people couldn't (verse 26). But Rabshakeh ignored them and instead got louder and more arrogant, even more intent on intimidating the people:

> *Then Rabshakeh stood and cried with a loud voice in the Jews' language, and spake, saying, Hear the word of the great king, the king of Assyria:*—2 Kings 18:28

Rabshakeh's message to the people was loud and clear: "You are powerless to stop me or what's about to happen. You can try, but nothing you can do will help. You're smaller and weaker. You don't have a chance."

TRUTH #2: YOU CAN MAKE A DIFFERENCE

Maybe you can relate to Hezekiah's situation here. Maybe in your life you've tried to silence the voice of the enemy only to hear it get louder and louder instead. Maybe you've tried to do what's right and tune out wrong influences, but it seems like it's harder than ever and nothing you can do will help. Well, that's exactly how Satan wants you to feel. He wants you to believe that no matter how hard you try, you can't make a difference. But the truth is that as a child of God, you don't have to rely on your own power. You can draw on the power of the Holy Spirit of God Almighty, the Creator of the universe. This is the same power that raised Jesus from the dead:

> *But if the Spirit of him that raised up Jesus from the dead dwell in you, he that raised up Christ from the dead shall also quicken your mortal bodies by his Spirit that dwelleth in you.*—ROMANS 8:11

And the truth is, with this power, you most certainly *can* make a difference. Jude said in the New Testament,

> *And of some have compassion, making a difference.*—JUDE 22

And Paul wrote,

And let us not be weary in well doing: for in due season we shall reap, if we faint not.—GALATIANS 6:9

The enemy wants you to believe that no matter how hard you try, you can't make a difference. But remember, God's ability to use you is not dependent on man's affirmation of you. It's not about what people think we are capable of, it's about what God says we are capable of. When Austin Gutwein was nine years old, he saw a movie about children in Africa who were orphaned when their parents died of AIDS. He wanted to do something to help, so he used his love of basketball to start a charity group called Hoops of Hope to raise money for these orphans. He raised $3,000 in his first year by just shooting free throws—2,057 free throws, to be exact, one for each African child who became orphaned every day. Today, Hoops for Hope has raised millions of dollars from people all over the world who have joined the cause. When asked what the experience taught him, Austin said he learned he really could make a difference: "This generation can step up and really change the world…and you don't have to wait to be an adult to do it."[1]

> God's ability to use you is not dependent on man's affirmation of you.

You can make a difference. Don't listen to the lies of the enemy.

LIE #3: YOU CAN'T TRUST GOD

Having made the people doubt their strength, Rabshakeh just kept going:

> *Thus saith the king, Let not Hezekiah deceive you: for he shall not be able to deliver you out of his hand: Neither let Hezekiah make you trust in the Lord, saying, The Lord will surely deliver us, and this city shall not be delivered into the hand of the king of Assyria.*—2 KINGS 18:29–30

Now he attacked their faith. He told them, "Don't listen to Hezekiah, because he's leading you astray. He told you your God can save you, but he's wrong. You can't trust your God." His goal in this taunt was to make them doubt God. Doubt is one of the most common tactics the enemy uses, probably because it can be very effective. Worse, doubt can be contagious and hard to overcome. Rabshakeh knew that if he could just get a few people to believe him and doubt the power of God, discouragement and defeat would spread throughout the people.

TRUTH #3: YOU CAN TRUST GOD FULLY

In 1999, John F. Kennedy, Jr. piloted his small plane from New York City to his family's home in Massachusetts to attend a wedding. With him on board were his wife, Caroline, and her sister. Kennedy was a licensed pilot but had not been approved to fly using only instruments to navigate. His takeoff was delayed until after dark, and Kennedy should've waited for daylight or enlisted the help of a more experienced pilot, but he decided to take off anyway. The plane crashed not long after killing all three passengers. Investigators later surmised Kennedy's inexperience had caused him to doubt the accuracy of his instrument panel and rely instead on his own faulty judgment despite the fact that he was flying in the dark over open water with no landmarks.[2] If he had just trusted his instruments, he might have been able to land safely.

Some of the greatest Christians to ever live have experienced seasons of doubt. The Bible is filled with stories of people who doubted God's promises would be fulfilled. Sarah, Abraham's wife, actually laughed when she heard that God would give her a son in her old age (Genesis 18). Gideon struggled with doubt, asking God for signs to prove He would be with the people in the fight against Midian (Judges 6). And Zacharias, who Luke 1 tells us was *"righteous in the sight of God, walking blamelessly in all the commandments and requirements of the Lord,"* still doubted he and his wife would have a child despite being directly visited by an angel of God with a message to this fact.

> So instead of letting doubt deter you, let it develop you.

Someone once said, "Sometimes we have to pass through the foyer of doubt in order to enter the sanctuary of certainty." Many times we have to experience doubt to learn the truth for ourselves: God is fully trustworthy. He never fails. He keeps all his promises. His Word is perfect, without error, and scientifically and historically accurate. So instead of letting doubt deter you, let it develop you and build your faith when you take your questions to the only One with all the answers. When you see for yourself that God does what He says He will do, you will understand why Joshua, Solomon, and others throughout history would praise God for His faithfulness.

> There failed not ought of any good thing which the Lord had spoken unto the house of Israel; all came to pass.—JOSHUA 21:45

> Blessed be the Lord, that hath given rest unto his people Israel, according to all that he promised: there hath not failed one word of all his good promise, which he promised by the hand of Moses his servant.—1 KINGS 8:56

LIE #4: FOLLOWING GOD'S PLAN LEADS TO MISERY

You'd think Rabshakeh would be tired of talking by now, but apparently he was chock full of hot air, because he wasn't done yet:

> Hearken not to Hezekiah: for thus saith the king of Assyria, Make an agreement with me by a present, and come out to me, and then eat ye every man of his own vine, and

every one of his fig tree, and drink ye every one the waters
of his cistern: Until I come and take you away to a land
like your own land, a land of corn and wine, a land of
bread and vineyards, a land of oil olive and of honey, that
ye may live, and not die: and hearken not unto Hezekiah,
when he persuadeth you, saying, The Lord will deliver us.
—2 KINGS 18:31–32

He told the people that they would be much better off surrendering to Assyria than hanging around with Hezekiah to follow God's plan; in fact, they would actually prosper. The problem with this was that earlier he had told them his plan was to come and take them away. Assyria didn't want to help Judah; they wanted to destroy them. Surrendering to Assyria meant surrendering to a life of slavery.

Satan wants you to believe God's plan for your life will only make you miserable compared to what he can offer you. He tells you everyone else is having way more fun than you, and if you'll only abandon God's plan, great things can happen and you'll be much happier. This is not only a lie; it's also a trap. It's a setup for heartache, disappointment, and destruction.

There is a way which seemeth right unto a man, but the
end thereof are the ways of death.—PROVERBS 14:12

TRUTH #4: FOLLOWING GOD'S PLAN BRINGS TRUE JOY

Take a stroll down the self-help section of your local Barnes & Noble, and you won't be able to go far without seeing dozens of books dedicated to helping you discover the "secret" to a life of happiness. In reality, there's no big mystery at all to finding true and lasting joy; the problem is, too many people go looking for it in all the wrong places.

Alexander the Great thought he could find happiness in achieving military glory. He was pretty awesome at it—he essentially conquered all the known world of his day. But instead of feeling fulfilled and satisfied, he felt empty. As the story goes, he cried in his tent because he had "no more worlds to conquer." The nineteenth century poet, Lord Byron, was sure happiness was found in living a life of self pleasure. He lived a life of excess and was famous for having numerous love affairs and racking up huge debts for his life of leisure. But at the end of his short life, he was far from happy, writing this line in a poem for his birthday: "The worm, the canker, and grief are mine alone."[3] And Voltaire, the famous eighteenth century writer and philosopher, didn't know where happiness could be found, but he tried hard to prove it wasn't found in God or Christianity. Yet, after years of looking for answers in Hinduism, Buddhism, and other philosophies, he came up empty.

If happiness can't be found in fame, money, or pleasure, where does it come from? Here's the truth: serving God and following His plan for our lives bring true joy and satisfaction. Our God wants the very best for us. He didn't design us to be miserable and would never ask us to follow Him into a life of misery. Look at what the Bible says about God's desires for us:

> *For I know the thoughts that I think toward you, saith the Lord, thoughts of peace, and not of evil, to give you an expected end.*—JEREMIAH 29:11

> *Delight thyself also in the Lord: and he shall give thee the desires of thine heart. Commit thy way unto the Lord; trust also in him; and he shall bring it to pass.*—PSALM 37:4–5

LIE #5: YOU CAN'T WIN

Rabshakeh saved what he thought was the most important part of his speech to Judah for very last. After telling the people that they couldn't trust God or Hezekiah and that being ruled by Assyria would be a vacation for them, he ended with this:

> *Hath any of the gods of the nations delivered at all his land out of the hand of the king of Assyria? Where are the gods of Hamath, and of Arpad? where are the gods of Sepharvaim, Hena, and Ivah? have they delivered Samaria out of mine hand? Who are they among all the*

gods of the countries, that have delivered their country out
of mine hand, that the Lord should deliver Jerusalem out
of mine hand?—2 KINGS 18:33–35

"You might as well give up right now," Rabshakeh was telling them. "Look at all the other nations we've conquered. Their gods couldn't save them, and yours can't save you. You can't stop us. You can't win." In case that sounded like empty bragging, consider this: archeologists have found Sennacherib's own account of wars with the nations Rabshakeh mentioned. In it, the king claimed to have destroyed 46 walled cities and taken over 200,000 captives. He had already marched down from the north to the Mediterranean coast to assert Assyrian authority. So everything pointed to Assyria's all-but-certain victory over Judah, too.

> Serving God and following His plan for our lives bring true joy and satisfaction.

TRUTH #5: YOU ARE VICTORIOUS IN CHRIST

Rabshakeh's goal was to make the people feel hopeless and that they had no chance of victory over Assyria. He saved this taunt for last because it would've been the most effective. He knew that when people lose all hope of victory, they truly are conquered.

In the same way, Satan uses this lie that you can't win against him to destroy your hope of ever overcoming sin and temptation.

Whatever you struggle with, he wants to convince you that no one has ever beat it, no one has ever conquered it, and you can never be free of your situation. He wants to break you and make you give up. But this lie overlooks one very important fact: if we have trusted in Christ for salvation, we don't have to fight our own battles. No matter how strong Satan may be, on his best day he's no match for Jesus.

> If we have trusted in Christ for salvation, we don't have to fight our own battles.

Rabshakeh was right when he said no other nation's god could save them, but he didn't count on Judah's God's being the Lord Almighty. In God's hands, Judah was already victorious. And the truth is, we don't have to be afraid of any enemy and we don't have to be a slave to any sin. In Christ we are more than conquerors.

> *For sin shall not have dominion over you: for ye are not under the law, but under grace.*—ROMANS 6:14

> *Nay, in all these things we are more than conquerors through him that loved us.*—ROMANS 8:37

> *I can do all things through Christ which strengtheneth me.*—PHILIPPIANS 4:13

So once Rabshakeh finally stopped talking, the people of Judah had a lot to think about, and they had a major decision to make. Second Kings 18:36 says they didn't say a word back to him because Hezekiah had commanded them not to—and we know in the Bible that silence is often the best response when opening your mouth can get you into trouble (Proverbs 10:19). But even though the people were quiet on the outside, I bet plenty of thoughts were swimming through their heads. They were facing an enemy who was bigger and stronger than they and who had already started to destroy Jerusalem's surrounding cities. On the one hand, they had Hezekiah who had tried his best to encourage them by telling them God had a plan, which they'd have to take on faith. But on the other hand, they could actually see the massive army of the enemy and hear Rabshakeh's taunts that no matter how hard they fought, they would certainly be next in a long line of nations that had been defeated. Which voice would they listen to?

The same choice is yours to make when you find yourself being intimidated by the enemy. The voice of Satan will tell you that your situation is hopeless, that you're worthless, and you can never win. But the voice of truth from the Word of God will tell you that you are fearfully and wonderfully made (Psalm 139:14), that God has big plans for your life (Jeremiah 29:11), and that through faith the victory is already yours.

Who will you believe?

4

+ +

THE STRUGGLE IS REAL

+ +

2 Kings 19:1–19

A few years ago, a slang phrase started appearing in memes and Vines and quickly became really popular in American culture. It's a phrase that I like to use because it fits so many situations. If you haven't used it yourself, you've at least heard someone tell you this: "The struggle is real." (I can see you nodding right now. You get it.) This phrase doesn't have an official dictionary definition, but we all understand the basic idea. It describes an unfortunate or tragic situation, and it's usually used ironically or sarcastically to add humor or drama because the situation really isn't all that terrible.

I'll give you an example. I love the restaurant Red Robin. Seriously. For me, it's the simple things in life, and believe it or not, Red Robin brings me joy. (Can I get an "Amen" for the bottomless steak fries?) So whenever Katie and I get a chance to go to Red Robin, it's automatically a good day. One weekend we made plans to have dinner at Red Robin, and I was excited. It was basically all I thought about all day long. I could practically taste those fries and the strawberry lemonade I was going to order along with them. But then something horrible happened. Actually, it's too terrible to even talk about, and I'm still a little traumatized even just recounting this memory for you. What happened was, sometime during the day, I yawned—just like any other day and any other yawn—and I heard something *pop* and then, for no reason at all, my jaw completely locked up. I couldn't open my mouth much wider than an inch without horrible sharp pain. I refused to give up on my dreams, so we still went to Red Robin that day, but I was probably the most miserable customer that had ever walked through the doors. To be in a position to eat as many french fries as I wanted….but not be able to open my mouth wide enough to fit them in and chew without pain? The struggle was real.

While we may use this phrase jokingly, I'm sure we all know people for whom a struggle was literally real. There are countless stories of people who endure horrible situations and struggle with unthinkable difficulties and challenges. It's enough that these people just survive their situations. But some manage not just to survive but to thrive and to become stronger and successful because of their struggles. You may not recognize the name Leonardo Del Vecchio, but I bet you know his products—RayBans and Oakleys. Did you know Leonardo grew up in an orphanage with his four siblings because their mother couldn't afford to care for them after their father died? When he was older, Leonardo worked in a factory that made molds for auto parts and eyeglasses, but the conditions were so bad that he lost part of his finger due to an accident on the job. He didn't let that stop him though; when he was twenty three, he opened his own glasses frame shop, which expanded over the years to six thousand retail stores, including the Sunglass Hut and LensCrafters chains.[1]

The actor Sylvester Stallone is another famous story of struggle. When his mother was in labor with him, the doctors had to remove baby Sly forcibly with forceps, but they slipped and damaged nerves in his face, which is why he talks the way he does. A product of divorce and a bad home environment, Sylvester was bullied by other kids and expelled from several schools for bad behavior. Later, when he was trying to make it big as an actor, Stallone wrote a screenplay for a movie called *Rocky* after being inspired by one of Muhammad Ali's boxing matches. He repeatedly submitted his script to agents and film executives but was rejected every time and told it just wasn't good enough. One person offered to buy the script from him if he'd consent to not being the star of the movie, but Stallone refused. Times were tough and Stallone was so broke that he eventually had to sell his beloved dog just to get $25 to survive. Finally, after some negotiation, he agreed to sell his script at a much lower price as long as he could still play the lead role, and the movie turned out to be a huge hit. In 1976, *Rocky* won the Oscar for Best Picture, and Stallone went on to star in five sequels and become a sought-after action star. (He also earned enough money to buy his dog back.)[2]

One of the trademark characteristics of a dark horse is that he or she endures times of struggle. And while Hezekiah wasn't an orphan and didn't have to sell his dog to get money for groceries, the struggle was real for him, too. Second Kings 19 is all about a letter that arrived at just the wrong moment in Hezekiah's life. His nation was under attack from Sennacherib and his people were being intimidated by Rabshakeh. To top it off, we'll see later that about this time, his health was also failing. Things were just not going Hezekiah's way. But through it all he remained strong.

> One of the trademark characteristics of a dark horse is that he or she endures times of struggle.

How is that possible? How did Hezekiah have the strength he needed not only to survive this challenging time but to thrive through it? See four things Hezekiah did that we should emulate if we are to learn how to be strong in times of struggle.

RESPOND WITH THE RIGHT SPIRIT

When I was in second grade, I got into the bad habit of getting "white notes." For those of you who didn't struggle with obedience in elementary school, a "white note" is something you get for misbehavior. Once you got a white note, your parents would have to sign it, acknowledging they understood their child had been disobedient. One particular day after receiving a white note, I let my emotions get the best of me. My teacher asked me to go outside, and I responded with this statement, " You can't tell me what to do, Miss Bossy!" After receiving another white note for my little outburst, we had a nice parent/teacher meeting to explain to me that was not the right response.

Maybe you've heard the saying, "Life is 10 percent what happens to you and 90 percent how you respond to it." We left off in 2 Kings 18 with Rabshakeh taunting the people of Judah and telling them they were about to lose the coming war over Jerusalem. In Chapter 19, news of this trash talk reaches Hezekiah, and we can learn some valuable lessons by the way he responded.

> *And it came to pass, when king Hezekiah heard it, that he rent his clothes, and covered himself with sackcloth, and went into the house of the Lord. And he sent Eliakim, which was over the household, and Shebna the scribe, and the elders of the priests, covered with sackcloth, to Isaiah the prophet the son of Amoz. And they said unto him, Thus*

saith Hezekiah, This day is a day of trouble, and of rebuke,
and blasphemy; for the children are come to the birth, and
there is not strength to bring forth. It may be the Lord thy
God will hear all the words of Rabshakeh, whom the king
of Assyria his master hath sent to reproach the living God;
and will reprove the words which the Lord thy God hath
heard: wherefore lift up thy prayer for the remnant that
are left.—2 KINGS 19:1–4

His Heart

Verse 1 of our text says that when Hezekiah heard what was going on, he *"rent his clothes, and covered himself with sackcloth."* This guy tore up his clothes, not in anger like the Hulk, but in grief. To hear that Sennacherib was not only going to attack him but that he was also blaspheming God? That really bothered Hezekiah. That tells you a lot about his heart. Hezekiah had a heart that loved God, and he was burdened when God's name was treated disrespectfully.

How do you react when you see or hear about sin around you—or when you sin yourself? Is your heart burdened? Or do you barely even notice? It's possible to get to a point in life where you're so desensitized to the prompting of the Holy Spirit that your heart is hardened, and you stop feeling convicted of sin. You just don't care anymore. This is what Paul called a "seared conscience" (1 Timothy 4:2), and it's a dangerous place for any believer to be.

The good news is, the damage can be undone by turning back to God.

Create in me a clean heart, O God; and renew a right spirit within me.—PSALM 51:10

His Humility

Have you ever gotten rubbed the wrong way by the tag of a t-shirt? It can be very irritating—super uncomfortable and scratchy. Why would clothing manufacturers place the tag in that exact spot so it constantly bothers your neck? (By the way, I think the people who came up with the idea of a tagless t-shirt are geniuses. All clothes should be tagless!)

Well, imagine that itchy feeling you get from the t-shirt tag, except it's all over your body—that's what it was like to wear sackcloth. So when the Bible says Hezekiah ripped his clothes and put on sackcloth instead, you know this was not something he did because none of his other clothes were clean. In Bible times, putting on sackcloth would often represent humility. It was humbling to wear because it made you look silly, and it was super uncomfortable. But it was also a symbol of repentance. By wearing it, Hezekiah was signifying that he realized it was his mistake that had led his nation to this point, and he was sorry. He was admitting his wrongdoing before God.

Are you someone who readily admits and repents when you've done wrong? Or do you stubbornly hold on to pride and resist correction?

> *But he giveth more grace. Wherefore he saith, God resisteth the proud, but giveth grace unto the humble.*—JAMES 4:6

His Hope

Hezekiah knew the only way through this trial was with the help of God, so he sent people to find the prophet Isaiah. His message for Isaiah was this: "Here's the situation. Please go to God with this. Maybe He will handle it." Hezekiah was hopeful that God wouldn't stand for His name being blasphemed and would step in to take care of the problem. He refused to stay discouraged because he knew God was able to help.

By the way, just as Hezekiah believed God would judge Sennacherib for what he'd been saying, you should also know and believe you will give an account to God—we all will—for every word you speak.

> *But I say unto you, That every idle word that men shall speak, they shall give account thereof in the day of judgment.*—MATTHEW 12:36

God holds us accountable for every lie, every curse word, every rumor, every little bit of gossip, every mean word or insult. Everything.

RUN TO GODLY INFLUENCES

In the spring of 2014, a ground flight crew at the Kahului airport in Maui watched in amazement as a teenage boy crawled out of the wheel well of a plane he'd been hiding in during a five-hour flight from San Jose, California. He had no identification or luggage—the only item he brought with him was a comb. But even more incredible than how the boy had gotten there was how he'd survived in the first place. The wheel well of a plane is a tiny, cramped space, and in high altitudes the boy would've had no oxygen and been subjected to below-freezing temperatures. The boy later told authorities he'd run away from his home and just thought Hawaii seemed like a nice place to visit.[3]

> You can learn a lot about someone by studying where he runs in times of difficulty.

You can learn a lot about someone by studying where he runs in times of difficulty. Where do you go when things get tough in your life? Do you run to a friend who is far from God? Do you keep to yourself and stop talking to everyone? Or do you, like the teenage stowaway, just try to find a nice place where you can hide away from it all for awhile?

Do you know where Hezekiah ran in difficulty? He ran to a prayer partner. He immediately sent word to Isaiah and asked him to pray. Second Chronicles 32 tells us that's exactly what Isaiah did:

> *And for this cause Hezekiah the king, and the prophet Isaiah the son of Amoz, prayed and cried to heaven.*
> —2 CHRONICLES 32:20

When times get tough and you want to get away, the best place to go is to someone who will listen to what's going on in your life and then will pray with you and direct you back to God. That's the measure of a good friend and a good sidekick—which is what every dark horse needs.

> *Iron sharpeneth iron; so a man sharpeneth the countenance of his friend.*—PROVERBS 27:17

When I think of sidekicks in the Bible, I remember Silas, who ministered with Paul on his missionary journeys. I think of the time Paul and Silas were beaten and thrown in prison for preaching the gospel. I know many of us would be pretty depressed at being in prison, but Silas was encouraging. Instead of complaining, he and Paul *"sang praises unto God"* (Acts 16:25).

Another time, Paul asked his friends at the church in Colossae to pray for him so he'd have the strength and opportunity to share the good news of Christ:

Withal praying also for us, that God would open unto us a
door of utterance, to speak the mystery of Christ, for which
I am also in bonds:— COLOSSIANS 4:3

If the apostle Paul, who was one of the greatest missionaries
and preachers the world has known, needed friends to pray for
and to encourage him, why would we think we're any different?

REMAIN CONFIDENT IN CHRIST

So Hezekiah's men went to see Isaiah and ask the prophet
to speak to God on the king's behalf, and he gave them an
encouraging message:

And Isaiah said unto them, Thus shall ye say to your
master, Thus saith the Lord, Be not afraid of the words
which thou hast heard, with which the servants of the king
of Assyria have blasphemed me. Behold, I will send a blast
upon him, and he shall hear a rumour, and shall return to
his own land; and I will cause him to fall by the sword in
*his own land.—*2 KINGS 19:6–7

Finally, Hezekiah heard some good news about this
Sennacherib situation. God was aware of what was happening, and
He had promised to take care of it. I'm sure Hezekiah must have
breathed a huge sigh of relief. But while Hezekiah was thanking
God for an answer to prayer, somewhere not too far away, another

challenge was brewing. In 2 Kings 19:8 we learn that Sennacherib had his own problems to deal with. Assyria was still fighting battles with other nations while they were trying to intimidate Judah (talk about multitasking!) which meant Sennacherib couldn't attack Jerusalem with the full strength of his kingdom just yet. But just because Sennacherib's fighting schedule was tied up at the moment didn't mean he couldn't attack Hezekiah in a different way. He wrote the king of Judah a nasty letter that let Hezekiah know exactly what Sennacherib thought of his faith and his God.

Over the years I've talked to many who begin to doubt what they believe when trouble strikes. Some challenge or difficulty will come into their lives, and their confidence in God will be shaken. It is no mistake that your faith is one of the first things the enemy will go after to weaken your defenses. Look at the two areas where Sennacherib wanted to cause Hezekiah to doubt his faith.

The Person of God

Sennacherib's letter started out pretty harshly:

> *Thus shall ye speak to Hezekiah king of Judah, saying, Let not thy God in whom thou trustest deceive thee, saying, Jerusalem shall not be delivered into the hand of the king of Assyria.*—2 Kings 19:10

He said, "If your God is telling you that I won't defeat you, let me tell you that's a lie. You can't trust your God—He's deceiving you." This isn't a new message. Satan and the world have tried to convince others that God isn't who He says He is since the beginning. And some people choose to believe this lie. Look at the Houston Texans running back Arian Foster, who defended his choice to be an atheist this way: "Everybody always says the same thing. You have to have faith. That's my whole thing: Faith isn't enough for me."[4]

The enemy can say what he wants to say, but the final word will always be God's, and in His Word we read:

> *And they that know thy name will put their trust in thee:*
> *for thou, Lord, hast not forsaken them that seek thee.*
> —PSALM 9:10

> *Wherefore God also hath highly exalted him, and given*
> *him a name which is above every name: That at the name*
> *of Jesus every knee should bow, of things in heaven, and*
> *things in earth, and things under the earth; And that every*
> *tongue should confess that Jesus Christ is Lord, to the glory*
> *of God the Father.*—PHILIPPIANS 2:9–11

The Promise of God

Sennacherib also wanted to make Hezekiah doubt that God's promise to deliver Judah from Assyria could be trusted (2 Kings 19:10). He wanted Hezekiah to believe God didn't mean what He'd said.

This tactic sounds pretty similar to how Satan tripped up Eve in the Garden of Eden, doesn't it? In Genesis 2, God told Adam not to eat fruit from the tree of the knowledge of good and evil, *"for in the day that thou eatest thereof thou shalt surely die"* (Genesis 2:17). But in Genesis 3, Satan got Eve to question what God had said:

> *Now the serpent was more subtil than any beast of the field which the Lord God had made. And he said unto the woman,* **Yea, hath God said,** *Ye shall not eat of every tree of the garden?*—GENESIS 3:1

Satan was saying, "Are you sure that's what God said? I don't know if that's true...." And the world does the same thing today when it comes to God's Word. When's the last time you heard someone challenge the Bible's accuracy and relevance? It happens all the time. People will try to get you to believe the Bible is old and outdated or just plain wrong. Some of their arguments sound valid enough to get you to question God's words. Let me tell you, that's a mistake. The Bible is reliable and trustworthy. The Bible has been proven true prophetically, historically, and scientifically.

> *Know therefore that the Lord thy God, he is God, the faithful God, which keepeth covenant and mercy with them that love him and keep his commandments to a thousand generations;*—DEUTERONOMY 7:9

God is not a man, that he should lie; neither the son of man, that he should repent: hath he said, and shall he not do it? or hath he spoken, and shall he not make it good? —NUMBERS 23:19

Every word of God is pure: he is a shield unto them that put their trust in him.—PROVERBS 30:5

All scripture is given by inspiration of God, and is profitable for doctrine, for reproof, for correction, for instruction in righteousness:—2 TIMOTHY 3:16

RELY ON THE POWER OF PRAYER

Have you ever been to a resort, perhaps for a family vacation or another type of trip? What makes resorts different from regular old hotels is that they're a sort of one-stop shop for all things relaxing and rejuvenating. Resorts will often have vacation packages that provide all the food and activities you could want during your stay so you rarely have to leave the property. But sometimes the cost of these vacations can be pretty ridiculous. I heard of one resort on an island in the Bahamas where you actually get to choose all the other resort guests during your stay. Of course, to get your choice, you have to also rent the entire island—for the low, low price of $37,000 *each night*. Seriously! Some of the resort's amenities are personalized fireworks shows and real life treasure hunts, but of course those aren't included in the regular price.[5]

There are many things we can do to relax and find rejuvenation after a tough day or during a trial, but I doubt most of us can afford to rent an island to do it. Do you know how Hezekiah did it? He went directly to God in prayer. I once heard a pastor say, "There's no such resort for the troubled soul as God Himself," and Hezekiah no doubt found that to be true. He knew there was no higher authority he could

> Prayer should be our foundation, not our fallback.

turn to for help, so he went straight to the source. Prayer should be our foundation, not our fallback. Instead of treating prayer like the last kid picked in a schoolyard kickball game, prayer should be our first pick, our top priority.

What I love about the way Hezekiah prayed is that it was so specific. God knows every single detail of our lives and our actions, so he knew exactly what was happening with Sennacherib. He knew every word of the letter that Hezekiah had just read. Yet Hezekiah picked up the pages of the letter and took them with him to the house of the Lord to pray. This wasn't just any old prayer; it was an amazing prayer. In it we find a pattern we can use for our own prayer lives.

Accuracy

Second Kings 19:14 says, "*And Hezekiah received the letter of the hand of the messengers, and read it: and Hezekiah went up into the house of the Lord, and **spread it before the Lord**.*" That's kind of an odd thing to do. What do you think might've been going through his mind? I think this was an act of surrender. By spreading out the pages of the letter before God, Hezekiah was saying, "I want to put it all on the table. I'll leave no detail out." By putting every word of the letter before the Lord, he could be specific in his prayer and get the details right; not just, "Lord, Sennacherib is saying some ugly things about You," but "Lord, here's exactly what he wrote." While it may not have been wise to tell everyone around him the details of this letter, he knew he could pour out his heart to God.

Where do you "spread" the details of the things that trouble you? Do you take them directly to the Lord? Or do you settle for just talking to your neighbors, friends, or coworkers?

Adoration

Hezekiah opened his prayer by acknowledging the greatness of God:

> *And Hezekiah prayed before the Lord, and said, O Lord God of Israel, which dwellest between the cherubims, thou art the God, even thou alone, of all the kingdoms of the earth; thou hast made heaven and earth.*—2 KINGS 19:15

When I was younger, I remember sometimes I'd come into the house from school or after playing with my friends with a burning question for my mom. I would hardly let her get a word in before I'd start telling her what I needed. Sometimes she'd just listen and give me an answer, but other times she'd stop me and say, "Well, hello to you, too" or "Hi mom, how was your day?" in the voice that meant this was what I was supposed to be saying to her. My mom's point was that it was rude to just approach her and start asking for things I needed without acknowledging the one who I needed them from. See, before giving God our requests, we need to give Him our reverence. Hezekiah needed something desperately from God, but he wasn't about to just jump in and start asking without showing that he knew exactly where his help was coming from.

> **Before giving God our requests, we need to give Him our reverence.**

Appeal

Next, Hezekiah asked for what he needed:

> *Lord, bow down thine ear, and hear: open, Lord, thine eyes, and see: and hear the words of Sennacherib, which hath sent him to reproach the living God.*—2 KINGS 19:16

What was the last thing you prayed really hard about? Too many times, teens are more concerned with asking for the latest gadgets or game systems or for the attention of someone they're interested in than in getting God's help with things that really matter. Hezekiah didn't plead with the Lord for a new iPhone or to finally get a girlfriend; he pleaded for God to answer and put a stop to sin.

Acknowledgment

In verses 17–18, Hezekiah admitted that Sennacherib was a dangerous enemy who had done everything he'd claimed, but there was one difference between Judah and those other nations:

> *Of a truth, Lord, the kings of Assyria have destroyed the nations and their lands, And have cast their gods into the fire: for they were no gods, but the work of men's hands, wood and stone: therefore they have destroyed them.*

The other nations worshipped false gods who were powerless to help them, and that's why they were defeated. Hezekiah acknowledged that the Lord was the only true God and that's why Jerusalem was still standing.

Aim

Hezekiah closed his prayer by telling God exactly what he hoped to get out of this situation:

> *Now therefore, O Lord our God, I beseech thee, save thou us out of his hand, that all the kingdoms of the earth*

may know that thou art the Lord God, even thou only.
—2 KINGS 19:19

Hezekiah's motivation was not fame or pride in his position. His only desire was to glorify the Lord before that heathen army. What motivates your prayers? Do you ask God for things that will only benefit you or the people you love? Or do you ask Him for things that will help you show others His love, grace, and salvation?

To me, one of the best parts about Hezekiah's prayer was what happened right after:

> *Then Isaiah the son of Amoz sent to Hezekiah, saying, Thus saith the Lord God of Israel, That which thou hast prayed to me against Sennacherib king of Assyria I have heard.*—2 KINGS 19:20

God heard Hezekiah's prayer. Isn't it amazing that we serve a God who not only knows everything about us but also wants to hear from us through prayer so He can meet our needs?

> *And this is the confidence that we have in him, that, if we ask any thing according to his will, he heareth us: And if we know that he hear us, whatsoever we ask, we know that we have the petitions that we desired of him.*—1 JOHN 5:14–15

Grayson Clamp was born with a condition that left him with a heart defect, no sight in one eye, and no hearing, as he was missing the auditory nerves that carry sound to the brain. In 2013, doctors successfully performed an experimental surgery that allowed Grayson to hear for the first time. (Look up and watch the video. I dare you not to be moved by it.) When Grayson heard his father speaking to him for the first time, he was so excited you could just see his eyes and his whole face light up with joy.[6]

Did you know our heavenly Father finds joy in hearing our voices? He delights in our communicating with him regularly through prayer. So then why do we sometimes go for days or longer without spending quality time with God in this way? Hezekiah knew that if he was to experience success in his time of struggle, it would only be as he drew closer to God through prayer. Spending that time with God gave him the strength he needed not just to survive Sennacherib's latest attack, but to thrive through it.

When's the last time you spent time with God to get His strength for your struggle?

5

+ +

HOOK IN THE NOSE

+ +

2 Kings 19:21–37

Did you grow up with sisters or brothers? If so, you know that one of the greater joys in life, at least when you're kids, is being able to push your siblings' buttons just for fun. I'm the youngest of four kids in my family, and I think I became a pro at getting on my siblings' nerves before I could even do my homework on my own. (Now *that's* talent.)

I remember one family vacation when we were doing a lot of driving and as usually happens when kids go on road trips, before long things were getting a little testy in the back seats of the car. By the time we finally pulled into a hotel to rest for the night, we were worn out and getting on each other's last nerves. My parents got themselves a room, probably to escape from us, and the four of us kids shared another room. We were all pretty tired so we turned the lights out and got in bed...and that's when something amazing happened.

I don't remember who started it, but my brother Larry and I discovered that when we rubbed our heads on the pillows, the friction created this crazy wave of blue electricity. True story. Pillow static electricity. (I dare you to say that's not the most awesome thing you've heard today.) So of course, there was no sleep to be had once we discovered this; it may have been 2:00 AM but just like that, we had our second wind. We could've gone on amusing ourselves indefinitely, but our sisters were becoming slightly irritated with us. (I can't imagine why.) Finally, my sister Kristine told us firmly, "Go to sleep!"

Go to sleep? Why would we want to be still and bring this supernatural, mystical phenomenon to an end? It just didn't seem like a logical choice.

Larry and I decided to show her our displeasure the best way we knew how—by giving her a shock. We rubbed our heads furiously against the pillows to build up the charge, and then we looked at each other in the dark, silently counted to three, jumped on our sisters' bed, and tackled Kristine. We felt the little shock as the electricity transferred to her and we laughed in glee. That would show her! We figured she'd be a little annoyed at first, but then she'd see how funny it was and try to get us back. But a few seconds went by, and Kristine wasn't moving and she wasn't laughing. In fact, she wasn't doing anything. She hadn't made a sound. Larry and I looked at each other. Had we underestimated the power of our combined static electricity super powers and accidentally electrocuted our sister? Our parents would never forgive us for this one.

We jumped off the bed and switched on a light to check out the situation more clearly. Thankfully, Kristine was still alive, but she looked far from okay. She was crying. Well, I guess you could call it crying, but it wasn't a regular cry; she had the tears but she wasn't making any noise. Maybe the electric shock had damaged her vocal chords? I was starting to get pretty nervous. We waited for her to say something to prove she was okay, and when she could finally speak, she sort of screeched the words that meant she'd reached the end of her rope, had no more patience, and had nothing left to give: "Just leave me *alone!*"

Have you ever been there? Maybe not to the shocked-silent-crying point, but to the point where you feel you've been pushed to your limit and you can't take much more? The point where you want your situation and the difficult people in your life to just leave you alone? I imagine that's how Hezekiah was feeling right about this time. After hounding Judah for years, the king of Assyria was intent on destroying Jerusalem. Even though Sennacherib couldn't be there himself to talk trash to Hezekiah, he'd sent his big-mouthed buddy Rabshakeh to scare Hezekiah's people with stories of all the other cities Assyria had destroyed and all the other people they'd killed. Then Sennacherib sent a letter mocking God to try to scare Hezekiah even more and to shake his faith. Now he and his army were on the outskirts of Jerusalem and getting ready to attack. Sennacherib was a problem that just wouldn't go away.

Sometimes it seems the struggles we face just won't go away, either. We find ourselves fighting the same sin over and over, long after we thought we were done with it. We discover the pain and hurt from a difficult time in our past is still lingering even years after it happened. We suffer from a health problem that just won't clear up. The longer we struggle, the more tired and frustrated we get, and the more we are tempted just to give up, thinking things will never get better. But I love the verses in our passage because in them we see Hezekiah finally experience victory. God heard Hezekiah's prayer from the first half of 2 Kings 19, and in this last half of the chapter He responded, teaching Hezekiah and us a valuable lesson: He is always in control.

> *But our God is in the heavens: he hath done whatsoever he hath pleased.*—PSALM 115:3

Sennacherib was one of the most powerful kings in the region, but he would soon find out that there was a much greater power than his: the power of God. In verse 28 of our passage, God comforted Hezekiah by saying He was going to *"put my hook in*

[Sennacherib's] *nose."* Talk about a word picture! He was saying, "I got this. I'm in control." When it seems that trials in your life are never going to end, and you have reached the end of your patience and your strength, remember these four statements and be comforted with the knowledge that God is in control in your life as well.

DON'T BECOME PROUD OVER WHAT GOD MADE POSSIBLE

As Isaiah begins to relay God's response to Hezekiah's prayer, what's immediately clear is that God knew exactly how much of a problem Sennacherib was. Sennacherib had been making some pretty bold declarations to brag about his power and might (2 Kings 19:23–24):

"My chariots are so awesome, they'll climb even the tallest mountain!"

"Nothing gets in my way; I cut the tallest and best trees down to get what I want."

"No water? No problem. I dig my own wells. It's my foot that dries up rivers; that's how powerful I am."

Have you ever met someone who was as arrogant as Sennacherib? At one time the famous boxer Muhammad Ali might have come pretty close, with his insistence that he was "the greatest" fighter in the history of the world, but even then I think

Sennacherib had Ali beat. He really thought he was all powerful and no one could stop him.

Here's the problem with arrogance. The Bible says that people who love to be exalted are pretty much guaranteed to be demoted.

Every one that is proud in heart is an abomination to the Lord: though hand join in hand, he shall not be unpunished.—PROVERBS 16:5

On a cold November day in 2012, a teenage girl walked into Cornerstone Bank in Waco, Nebraska, with a pillowcase and handed a note to a teller that said, "You're being robbed. No ink bags, no alarms. You have two minutes." Less than a minute later and about $6,000 richer, the young bank robber made her escape. The bank employees later gave police an accurate description of the girl and her getaway car, but as it turned out, the police didn't really need help finding her. The next day, the girl—nineteen-year-old Hannah Sabata— uploaded a YouTube video titled "Chick Bank Robber" in which she admitted to the robbery and auto theft while wearing the exact same clothes she'd worn during the robbery, which was caught on surveillance cameras. Sabata fanned herself with the stolen cash in front of the camera and held up notes bragging that she was now rich. The video quickly went viral, and Hannah was arrested

> The Bible says that people who love to be exalted are pretty much guaranteed to be demoted.

just hours after it was uploaded, the police having also received a call from Hannah's ex-boyfriend, who Hannah had texted to brag about what she'd done.[1]

Just like Hannah, who is probably one of the worst bank robbers in the world, Sennacherib had a problem with boasting. But he was about to get a wake-up call.

> *Hast thou not heard long ago how I have done it, and of ancient times that I have formed it? now have I brought it to pass, that thou shouldest be to lay waste fenced cities into ruinous heaps. Therefore their inhabitants were of small power, they were dismayed and confounded; they were as the grass of the field, and as the green herb, as the grass on the house tops, and as corn blasted before it be grown up.*—2 Kings 19:25–26

God was telling Sennacherib, "Everything you think you accomplished? I did it all. You think you're so great, but I allowed you to have those chariots and I gave you those soldiers. You thought you conquered those nations because you're so powerful, but I made that possible. Everything you have came from Me."

We must realize—hopefully long before we get ourselves into trouble—that anything and everything good in our lives comes from God. Many people get too caught up in their accomplishments and start feeling as if they "deserve" and have "earned" good things. Be careful not to follow this mindset. Sure, you may have worked hard for something, but don't forget who gave you your intelligence, your talent, and your ability to work, not to mention your very life. Don't become proud over what God made possible.

NOT ONLY IS GOD AWARE, HE IS ACTIVE

The next words God spoke through Isaiah are some of my favorites in this passage:

> *But I know thy abode, and thy going out, and thy coming in, and thy rage against me.*—2 KINGS 19:27

This is kind of an odd verse to be a favorite, but let me explain what's so great about these words. Here God was telling Sennacherib and Hezekiah, "I know."

To Sennacherib God was saying, "I know you. I know where you live, and I know what you've been saying. I know it all." And with these words He was indirectly telling Hezekiah, "I know everything that's going on. None of it is a surprise to Me." This would have been such an encouragement to Hezekiah. He'd been worried and discouraged because the enemy was terrorizing his people, and through it all to that point, God had been relatively quiet. Hezekiah had been hoping for a sign, any sign, to let him know that God was aware. I can imagine what his mindset might have been as he wrote to Isaiah and sent men to inquire, "Have you had any word from God yet? Any news? Anything?" but heard nothing.

But then God spoke, and His words were refreshing and calmed Hezekiah's spirit. He didn't need to worry. God had been listening and He knew exactly what was happening—in fact, He knew more about the situation than Hezekiah did. Did you notice that none of the things Sennacherib boasted about in 2 Kings 19:23–24 were in the letter he'd sent to Hezekiah? Hezekiah didn't even know the extent of Sennacherib's arrogance. But God knew.

God knows more than we think He does. We'll hear and say things like, "God is everywhere and He sees it all," but I think there are times we don't really believe it. Sometimes I think we're tempted to believe when things are going wrong in our lives that God is nowhere to be found and has no idea what we're going through. But God doesn't just know the *existence* of our problems; He knows the full *extent* of our problems.

> We must realize—hopefully long before we get ourselves in trouble—that anything and everything good in our lives comes from God.

> *Talk no more so exceeding proudly; let not arrogancy come out of your mouth: for the Lord is a God of knowledge, and by him actions are weighed.*—1 SAMUEL 2:3

> *For he looketh to the ends of the earth, and seeth under the whole heaven;*—JOB 28:24

Not too long ago, my brother Larry told me his wife Ashley had been at their home alone with their baby when something pretty alarming happened. A couple of strange men approached the house and started peering in the windows and banging on the door. Ashley was pretty concerned when she realized these guys were getting ready to rob her home, so she called my brother. But little did she know, Larry was already on his way. No, he doesn't have some sort of superhuman ability to sense danger. A few weeks earlier, he'd installed a new security system with cameras and alerts to let him know whenever anything suspicious was happening at his house. He'd gotten an alert before Ashley had even noticed the men outside, and he made it home in time to scare them off.

> Many times we can be concerned or even overwhelmed in the midst of our difficulties when God is already in motion to deliver us.

Many times we too can be concerned or even overwhelmed in the midst of our difficulties when God is already in motion to deliver us. He is already working behind the scenes, well aware of what's going on. And this is exactly what happened with Sennacherib. In 2 Kings 19:28, we see God already had a plan for how to handle him:

Because thy rage against me and thy tumult is come up into mine ears, therefore I will put my hook in thy nose, and my bridle in thy lips, and I will turn thee back by the way by which thou camest.—2 KINGS 19:28

God had had enough of Sennacherib's boasting. The hook and bridle were tools that would've been used to tame or control an animal, to let it know who was master. God used these images here to show He intended to demonstrate that He, not the Assyrian king, was really in control. God was letting Hezekiah know that not only was He aware of the problem, He was going to do something about it—according to His timetable.

Did you know the Bible never once tells us that when we have difficulties or trials, we're just supposed to "figure it out" on our own? Instead, we read over and over that we need to trust God. Why do you think that is? Because He's already got it all figured out.

> *Fear thou not; for I am with thee: be not dismayed; for I am thy God: I will strengthen thee; yea, I will help thee; yea, I will uphold thee with the right hand of my righteousness.*—Isaiah 41:10

TO BEAR FRUIT UPWARD, TAKE ROOT DOWNWARD

Next, God through Isaiah says something pretty interesting:

> *And the remnant that is escaped of the house of Judah shall yet again take root downward, and bear fruit upward.*
> —2 Kings 19:30

He was telling Hezekiah that the kingdom of Judah would one day bear fruit again. It would be built back up and experience success. But first, the people had to take root downward. They'd have to get rooted and established in order to grow. And that's always the process for growth in our lives. If we want fruit, we have to start with our foundation.

I really enjoy the game of golf. I'm not going to say my game has Tiger Wood's status, but I don't think anyone would be too embarrassed to be seen with me on a green. (Okay, maybe you would.) When I first started playing, I had trouble hitting the ball straight. I'd line everything up and concentrate super hard, I'd picture the ball slicing straight through the air, and I'd practice my swing, but no matter what I did, I couldn't follow through with a straight shot. Finally, a friend told me what I was doing wrong. "Your footwork is off," he told me. "You swing so hard that you spin, and that throws off your shot. If you get the footwork right, the rest of your body will follow through." I took my friend's advice and found to my surprise that he was right. Everything started at the foundation.

In the same way, if you want spiritual blessings in your life, you must build a solid base. You must get rooted in the Word of God.

> *Rooted and built up in him, and stablished in the faith, as ye have been taught, abounding therein with thanksgiving.*
> —COLOSSIANS 2:7

Study to shew thyself approved unto God, a workman that needeth not to be ashamed, rightly dividing the word of truth.—2 TIMOTHY 2:15

This book of the law shall not depart out of thy mouth; but thou shalt meditate therein day and night, that thou mayest observe to do according to all that is written therein: for then thou shalt make thy way prosperous, and then thou shalt have good success.—JOSHUA 1:8

Charles Spurgeon told a story about a Roman Catholic priest who rebuked a young woman and her brother for reading the Bible. He asked, "How could you read such a bad book?" The woman told the priest that her brother used to be a gambler and a drunkard living a wicked life, but since he'd begun reading the Bible, he had a steady job, had quit drinking, and had started giving to help the poor. She asked him, "How could such a bad book produce such good fruits?"[2]

> If we want fruit, we have to start with our foundation.

Sometimes we want the benefits and blessings of right living, but we're not willing to do the work of establishing the foundation. But when's the last time you saw a tall, strong, fruit-bearing tree that had no root system beneath the ground? In the same way, we cannot bear fruit in our lives without spending time in the Word of God and in prayer.

God was telling Hezekiah that things were going to start looking much better for Judah, but the people needed to get rooted first. They needed to rededicate themselves to the Lord and recommit to living for Him only.

Is your life fruitful? Are you steadily growing and progressing in your walk with Christ? If not, better check your foundation.

OUR GRIEF SETS THE STAGE FOR GOD'S GLORY

Dr. Paul Brand was a pioneering medical missionary known for his work with lepers and for transforming social conceptions about the progression of leprosy. It was thought for many centuries that leprosy (more formally known as Hansen's Disease) caused rotting of the flesh that made victims' feet or fingers fall off. After working for years with those suffering from leprosy, however, Dr. Brand discovered that rotting flesh wasn't the cause at all. Instead, the problem was that leprosy causes victims to lose feeling in the body parts affected by the disease. Because they can't feel pain, lepers often don't know when they are injured and can sometimes wear away a wounded body part without knowing it. For this reason, Dr. Brand, author of several books including *The Gift of Pain,* came to believe that pain has an express purpose. He wrote, "God designed the human body so that it is able to survive *because* of pain… If I

> We need to remember that God has a purpose behind our pain.

had the power to eliminate pain, I would not exercise that right. Its value is too great."[3]

We need to remember that God has a purpose behind our pain. Hezekiah had suffered under the threat of Assyria for years, and his father had before him as well, but there was a reason behind it all. God was setting the stage to bring a great delivery of His people.

God's Passion

In 2 Kings 19:31 we read,

> *For out of Jerusalem shall go forth a remnant, and they that escape out of mount Zion: the zeal of the Lord of hosts shall do this.*—2 KINGS 19:31

According to Merriam-Webster, the word *zeal* means "eagerness and ardent interest in pursuing something."[4] Another word for this is *passion*. God was passionate about pursuing and preserving His people. What are you passionate about? If you're having trouble thinking of something, let me suggest that a good place to start would be passion for the things of God. We ought to care about the things He cares about. We ought to have a heart like David's:

> *O God, thou art my God; early will I seek thee: my soul thirsteth for thee, my flesh longeth for thee in a dry and thirsty land, where no water is;*—PSALM 63:1

God's Protection

Have you ever prayed for God to act in a situation and then wondered just how He would do it? I'm sure Hezekiah had some questions about how God would deliver Judah from the king of Assyria. But in the next verses in 2 Kings 19 God tells Hezekiah His plan:

> *Therefore thus saith the Lord concerning the king of Assyria, He shall not come into this city, nor shoot an arrow there, nor come before it with shield, nor cast a bank against it. By the way that he came, by the same shall he return, and shall not come into this city, saith the Lord. For I will defend this city, to save it, for mine own sake, and for my servant David's sake.*—2 KINGS 19:32–34

Sennacherib talked a good game, but God told Hezekiah that not a single one of his arrows would enter Jerusalem. How cool is that? Hezekiah and his people were completely protected. Did you know that, as a child of God, when you are following His will you have access to the same kind of protection? Many times people think that God's will is scary, but the truth is, the safest place you could ever be in life is in the center of His will. God looks out for His children in ways we can't see or imagine.

God's Power

The rest of the chapter gets kinda crazy. Watch how God put His plan into action:

And it came to pass that night, that the angel of the Lord went out, and smote in the camp of the Assyrians an hundred fourscore and five thousand: and when they arose early in the morning, behold, they were all dead corpses. So Sennacherib king of Assyria departed, and went and returned, and dwelt at Nineveh. And it came to pass, as he was worshipping in the house of Nisroch his god, that Adrammelech and Sharezer his sons smote him with the sword: and they escaped into the land of Armenia. And Esarhaddon his son reigned in his stead.—2 KINGS 19:35–37

You remember when Sennacherib was boasting about the size of his army, right? The Bible says an angel came through the Assyrian camp in the night and killed 185,000 men. All of those men were no match for one angel of God. That's some serious power. When Sennacherib woke up the next morning to find that his men were dead, I bet all his bragging about how powerful he was suddenly seemed pretty pointless. With no army left to fight Jerusalem, Sennacherib ran off—but God wasn't done with him yet. While he was worshipping one of his false gods, his own sons sneaked up on him and killed him. What a sad end for a guy who thought he was stronger than the Almighty God!

> The safest place you could ever be in life is in the center of His will.

God kept His promise and delivered Hezekiah from the hands of the Assyrians, and from this we should learn that God is very present in our own difficulties. Hezekiah couldn't see God's plan from his perspective of suffering, but that didn't mean God didn't

> Many times our greatest difficulty is simply paving the way for God's greatest delivery.

have a plan. In fact, just when things were looking bleakest for Hezekiah, God was simply setting the stage for a huge victory. Hezekiah didn't have to lift a finger in his own defense; God had everything handled. In the same way, many times our greatest difficulty is simply paving the way for God's greatest delivery. Keep

this in mind the next time you're dealing with a tough situation that seems like it will never go away. Sometimes it's just a matter of having the right perspective.

> *It is better to trust in the Lord than to put confidence in man.*—PSALM 118:8

Trust God. Trust that He knows exactly what you're going through, and just like with Hezekiah, He's had a plan all along.

6

+ +

THE HEART OF A DARK HORSE

+ +

2 Kings 19:21–37

On September 6, 1986, two Russian ships collided in the Black Sea in a tragic accident that was one of the worst in the country's history. One of the ships, a freighter carrying a load of oats, was lightly manned, but the other, a 17,000-ton, 525-foot liner, was carrying 1,234 people. Although there was almost no damage to the freighter, the liner was ripped apart and started to sink within fifteen minutes of the collision, leaving no time for the crew to launch lifeboats. Nearly 400 people drowned in the accident, which investigators later determined could've been completely avoided. Neither ship had malfunctioning technology, and there were no weather conditions that could have been responsible. Instead, the accident was due to human pride. The captains of both ships knew they were on a collision course at least forty-five minutes before impact, and they could have steered clear of each other, but they trusted instead in their own skill and refused to yield to each other—in fact, the freighter captain sent a message that essentially said, "I got this." Both men were later arrested and charged with gross negligence and carelessness.[1]

In our study of the life of Hezekiah, we've learned some valuable lessons about what it means to be a dark horse. It means taking opportunities to overcome obstacles. It means not letting fear eliminate your fight or letting the enemy shake your confidence. It means going to God to find strength when challenges arise and trusting that He's working even when things look darkest. But

> A true dark horse knows that overcoming obstacles and finding confidence and strength to rise to victory are not solo acts.

one of the most important dark horse qualities I hope you take from this study is this: the heart of a dark horse is full of humility, not pride. You see, a true dark horse knows that overcoming obstacles and finding confidence and strength to rise to victory are not solo acts. They are made possible because of the power and grace of God.

Hezekiah had to learn about humility in a very unique way. Remember in Chapter 4 when we were talking about struggle, and I told you one reason Sennacherib's letter arrived at just the wrong time was because Hezekiah was also having health problems? Well, chronologically our passage in 2 Kings 20 occurs at the same time as those verses in 2 Kings 19, which means it was still the fourteenth year of Hezekiah's reign, the army of Assyria hadn't been destroyed yet, and Sennacherib was still alive. Although we know that God delivered Judah and put Sennacherib in his place, Hezekiah hadn't seen these miracles yet. All he knew was that this fourteenth year was a pretty terrible year.

Have you ever experienced a fourteenth year in your life? A time when it seemed like problems were just piling up on top of each other and everything was coming at you all at once? I remember a few years ago when it certainly seemed that way for my family. In a short span of time my brother Larry got cancer, my dad became very sick, and my sister Danielle—who had just had a baby—suddenly broke her knee. I remember thinking, as it seemed like every few days we got another call with more bad news, *What else can go wrong?*

Between 2 Kings 19 and 20, Hezekiah's problems just kept piling up. He was dealing with the threat of Assyria's surrounding Jerusalem, his people's panicking and losing confidence, and Sennacherib and Rabshakeh's mocking his faith in God and promising to decimate his land...and then to top it all off, he got sick. But the Bible says that Hezekiah wasn't just dealing with a mild illness; he was *"sick unto death"* (2 Kings 20:1). We don't know what he had, but verse 7 mentions a "boil," which in the Hebrew language indicates an inflammation or ulcer that would've been extremely painful.[2] He was so sick and in so much pain that he was basically bedridden, and he cried to the Lord for help.

Did you know that God is aware of and concerned with our pain? David wrote that God keeps a record of every time we cry:

> *Thou tellest my wanderings: put thou my tears into thy bottle: are they not in thy book?*—PSALM 56:8

God is concerned about us. He loves us. As we saw in the last chapter, He has a purpose behind our pain. John Butler said it this way: "At such times we may think God has forsaken us. But God has not forsaken us. He has simply allowed us to experience troubles piled upon troubles in order to strengthen our faith in him."[3] And God hadn't forsaken Hezekiah, either. But Hezekiah had one last lesson to learn through these trials. Let's take a look at how Hezekiah learned humility, and some steps we must take if we too are going to develop the heart of a dark horse.

EVALUATE YOUR TIME

If someone could tell you the exact date when you would die, would you want to know? Some people pay fortune tellers or psychics who pretend to know the future or who claim the lines in your palms can tell them how long you have to live, but we know that stuff's bogus. Only God knows the time of our death because He's the one that appointed it.

> *And as it is appointed unto men once to die, but after this the judgment:*—HEBREWS 9:27

> *Seeing [man's] days are determined, the number of his months are with thee, thou hast appointed his bounds that he cannot pass;*—JOB 14:5

But let's just imagine someone could tell you when you would die. Let's say that, like Hezekiah, you were very sick and the doctors said you had only weeks to live. How would you respond? Many people would start to reflect on how they spend their time. We all realize to a certain degree that life doesn't last forever, yet we tend to behave as if we have all the time in the world. But if you read stories of people who have found out their time is running short, you'll notice one thing they have in common is they suddenly start to realize how precious time is and how much of it they've been wasting on things that don't matter.

Studies have suggested that in the average American lifespan of seventy-eight years, more than a quarter of it—twenty-five years—is spent sleeping; nine years are spent watching TV; and in some cities over three months, or about forty-two hours every year, are spent just sitting in traffic.[4] And that's not even the worst of it. A late 2015 study by Common Sense Media found that tweens and teens spend between six and nine hours every day on social media, sometimes checking their social media profiles up to 100 times *per day*. That's even more time than the average person spends sleeping![5] And in the last few years companies like Hulu and Netflix have made millions by providing streaming media that take up even more of our free time, leading to a January 2016 study that showed each Netflix subscriber spent an average of 568 hours streaming and binge watching shows in 2015.[6] If you knew you were about to die, how much of that time would suddenly seem like a waste?

> The best players always keep an eye on the clock.

I remember one basketball game I played in high school when there were about ten seconds left on the game clock, and we were up by just one point. I inbounded the ball to my teammate, expecting him to start our next play so we could maintain our lead, but instead he threw the ball up in the air as high as he could and raised his hands in victory. The ball went out of bounds and to the other team, and I looked at my teammate in shock. He'd just given up our chance. What was he doing? He explained that he'd misread how much time we had left: "I thought the clock said one second, not ten." Luckily, we still won the game, but my friend learned an important lesson: the best players always keep an eye on the clock.

So teach us to number our days, that we may apply our hearts unto wisdom.—PSALM 90:12

Redeeming the time, because the days are evil. —EPHESIANS 5:16

The truth is, in life there is no visible game clock. We don't know how much time we have left. But Hezekiah knew his time was nearly up. God's message through Isaiah was, *"set thine house in order; for thou shalt die, and not live"* (2 Kings 20:1). By that he meant, "You're going to die from this sickness. You need to prepare for your death." Hezekiah needed to get busy putting some things in motion—probably things like getting his finances in order, making sure his family

> The truth is, in life there is no visible game clock.

was taken care of, and equipping the next king of Judah to pick up where he'd left off in defending the country against Assyria. But most importantly, Hezekiah needed to prepare himself to meet God.

Are you prepared to meet God? What if you died today? Do you know for sure where you would spend eternity? There's a way you can know that when you meet God it will be on happy terms.

That if thou shalt confess with thy mouth the Lord Jesus, and shalt believe in thine heart that God hath raised him from the dead, thou shalt be saved. For with the heart man believeth unto righteousness; and with the mouth confession is made unto salvation.—ROMANS 10:9–10

For God so loved the world, that he gave his only begotten Son, that whosoever believeth in him should not perish, but have everlasting life.—JOHN 3:16

Some people hear this good news and say, "Yeah, I want to go to Heaven when I die. But I'll make that decision later. I need more time first." The problem is not that we need more time; it's that we need to use our time better. None of us have any guarantees of a long life. In fact, we don't even know that we'll be alive tomorrow.

Whereas ye know not what shall be on the morrow. For what is your life? It is even a vapour, that appeareth for a little time, and then vanisheth away.—JAMES 4:14

The time God has given you right now is what matters. If you've been putting off giving your life to Christ and accepting His sacrifice on the cross to give you the gift of eternal life and forgiveness of sins, do it now.

…behold, now is the accepted time; behold, now is the day of salvation.—2 CORINTHIANS 6:2

Every year when I was growing up, my dad would host a retreat for the staff of our church, and they'd all get away for a few days to be refreshed and get some training to prepare for the year to come. I always loved retreat times because other staff kids would come to stay at my house with a babysitter while all our parents were away. It was basically just days of non-stop fun with some of my best friends. Before my parents left, they would give us one instruction: "Keep the house clean." One of my favorite things to do with my friends was build tents, and one year after my parents left we decided to build the mother of all tents. We literally used dozens of sheets, grabbing them from my mother's linen cabinets and off all of the beds in the house. My brother helped us come up with the master design, and we got started.

We moved all the furniture in the house and made tunnels, hallways, and individual rooms, all out of sheets. We moved our TVs and PlayStation into our tent rooms and played video games, and when we were tired of that, we started a game of Cowboys and Indians and chased each other through our sheet hallways and tunnels. I had my favorite BB gun, and everything was going great—until I shot one of my friends in the neck from about a foot away. Whoops! I didn't realize the gun was loaded until my friend started bleeding. Luckily, my gun wasn't that powerful, but my buddy was still hurt and crying, and what had been a wonderful time with the guys was quickly turning pretty messy...and then to make it worse, my parents walked in the door, home much earlier than expected.

I can only imagine what went through their minds as they took in what we'd done to the house: dozens of sheets everywhere, the furniture all askew and toys lying everywhere, a boy running around crying and bleeding, and me holding the BB gun, looking guilty. Needless to say, our party was over. We'd had one job: to keep the house clean. But we'd gotten caught up in our own world and lost track of time, and suddenly the time we thought we had to get our house in order was cut short.

Someday your time will be cut short. Are you prepared? Are you using the time you have now to live for God? Have you made your personal commitment to Him? If not, get that settled *today*. There's no time to waste.

ELIMINATE PRIDE

There's nothing quite like a devastating illness or personal problem to give perspective and show us that we are not in control. When he heard he would soon die, Hezekiah *"turned his face to the wall, and prayed unto the LORD"* (2 Kings 20:2). He prayed a prayer that most of us would consider self-righteous:

> *I beseech thee, O Lord, remember now how I have walked before thee in truth and with a perfect heart, and have done that which is good in thy sight. And Hezekiah wept sore.*—2 KINGS 20:3

He prayed, "God, why me? Why now? I haven't done anything wrong; in fact, I've been a good person! Look at everything I've done!" But I don't think Hezekiah was being self-righteous. I think he was expressing natural human emotions that any of us would in the same circumstance. It always seems somehow more unfair whenever bad things happen to good people. While he'd made mistakes in his life, Hezekiah was a good, faithful, and upright man. He wept (verse 3) because he knew his job as king of Judah wasn't done yet—Sennacherib hadn't been defeated and his people weren't safe. Hezekiah wanted more time.

> **Are you using the time you have now to live for God?**

In answer to his request, God sent Isaiah to Hezekiah with some great news:

> *Turn again, and tell Hezekiah the captain of my people, Thus saith the Lord, the God of David thy father, I have heard thy prayer, I have seen thy tears: behold, I will heal thee: on the third day thou shalt go up unto the house of the Lord. And I will add unto thy days fifteen years; and I will deliver thee and this city out of the hand of the king of Assyria; and I will defend this city for mine own sake, and for my servant David's sake.*—2 KINGS 20:5–6

Notice the end of verse 6 where God said he would heal Hezekiah and rescue Judah "*for mine own sake, and for my servant David's sake.*" God was going to give him extra time, but just in case there was any confusion, He wasn't doing it because Hezekiah was a good person or had done such great things in his life. God said, "I'm doing this because of who *I* am. I'm going to heal you for *My* glory."

We need to remember that God's promises are based on who He is, not who we are. The apostle Paul knew this, writing to the church in Corinth:

> *But by the grace of God I am what I am: and his grace which was bestowed upon me was not in vain; but I laboured more abundantly than they all: yet not I, but the grace of God which was with me.*—1 CORINTHIANS 15:10

If you've been saved, you have received the free gift of salvation. You have received the grace of God, and as a result, you have access to His blessings and promises. But these aren't based on what we can do or what we bring to the table. They are available to us because of what God has already done.

> *But he giveth more grace. Wherefore he saith, God resisteth the proud, but giveth grace unto the humble.*—JAMES 4:6

What followed next was a miracle. In 2 Kings 20:7–11, God used figs to heal Hezekiah's body of the painful boils. Then to confirm His promise to extend Hezekiah's life, God caused the shadow of the sun dial of Ahaz to move backward, which would only have been possible through supernatural intervention. This miraculous healing and restoration were reminders that God was greater than Hezekiah's circumstances and that his condition was not his conclusion. The same can be said of you. I don't know what circumstances you may be facing, but I do know that God is greater. Do you believe that?

EXCLAIM THE GOODNESS OF GOD

So if you're Hezekiah and you've just been divinely healed from a sickness that was about to kill you, what's your next move? Every time I think about how Hezekiah must have woken up the next morning knowing he had been given a second chance at life, I think about the Christmas movie, "It's a Wonderful Life." At the end of the movie, when George Bailey takes back his wish that he'd never been born and returns home, he can't contain his joy. He runs through the town with a huge grin, shouting "Merry Christmas!" to everyone he sees. George is full of gratitude for his second chance, and he uses it to show his family and friends how much they mean to him.

> We need to remember that God's promises are based on who He is, not who we are.

If you read the next verses in our passage, you'll notice Hezekiah responded to his second chance at life in a much different way than George Bailey. The Bible says that the king of Babylon and his son asked about Hezekiah's health, and instead of telling them how grateful he was to God for healing him and blessing him, Hezekiah was filled with pride.

> *And Hezekiah hearkened unto them, and shewed them all the house of his precious things, the silver, and the gold, and the spices, and the precious ointment, and all the house of his armour, and all that was found in his treasures: there was nothing in his house, nor in all his dominion, that Hezekiah shewed them not. Then came Isaiah the prophet unto king Hezekiah, and said unto him, What said these men? and from whence came they unto thee? And Hezekiah said, They are come from a far country, even from Babylon. And he said, What have they seen in thine house? And Hezekiah answered, All the things that are in* **mine** *house have they seen: there is nothing among* **my** *treasures that I have not shewed them.*—2 KINGS 20:13–15

Hezekiah missed an opportunity to give God glory. Babylon was not a nation of people who loved God, which meant this was a prime chance for Hezekiah to witness to them about everything God had done for him and for Judah. He could have shown them evidence of God's grace, but instead he took them to his trophy case, bragging about his accomplishments and everything he owned—which, by the way, were only made possible because of God. Instead of exclaiming the goodness of God, he exalted himself.

One of the strange habits of the human heart is to feel proud about what we've received by grace. Many times we also take credit for things we had nothing to do with. I remember when I was in elementary school, I wanted to participate in a schoolwide drawing contest. Whoever could draw the best picture of our new church building would win a prize. Now, I had the desire to win, but my artistry skills were a little lacking. But my brother is pretty talented, so I asked him to draw for me. When he finished, I proudly displayed "my" drawing in the church hallway for all to see. The plan worked great—that is, until my mom saw my drawing. You see, she'd been around awhile, and she knew me pretty well. She knew I was no artist. She told me, "Someone else had to have drawn that. It's too good for you to have done it on your own." Basically she was saying, "Matt, I know you can't draw, you loser!"

One of the strange habits of the human heart is to feel proud about what we've received by grace.

I'm kidding a little bit in that my mom would never call me a loser, but you get the point, right? I was trying to take credit for something my Mom knew I was not capable of doing. I was trying to make myself look good instead of the person who was really responsible. And Hezekiah's misplaced priorities allowed him to try to make himself look good instead of pointing the king of Babylon to the One who was really responsible. He was stealing glory that rightfully belonged to God.

What are you proud of? Have you given the credit to God?

For who maketh thee to differ from another? and what hast thou that thou didst not receive? now if thou didst receive it, why dost thou glory, as if thou hadst not received it?—1 CORINTHIANS 4:7

Every good gift and every perfect gift is from above, and cometh down from the Father of lights, with whom is no variableness, neither shadow of turning.—JAMES 1:17

Whenever good things happen in our lives, we should use them as opportunities to show others not how awesome we are, but how good our God is. He wants others to look at us and see Him so that they'll say, "Wow, God must have been involved. This must be His doing. Let's give Him all the praise."

There was a price to pay for Hezekiah's lack of humility. God sent Isaiah back to the king with another message:

Behold, the days come, that all that is in thine house, and that which thy fathers have laid up in store unto this day, shall be carried into Babylon: nothing shall be left, saith the Lord. And of thy sons that shall issue from thee, which thou shalt beget, shall they take away; and they shall be eunuchs in the palace of the king of Babylon.
—2 KINGS 20:17–18

Hezekiah's action impacted his sons and future generations. This was a steep price! Have you heard of the term *collateral damage?* It's a term used when unintentional harm is inflicted on an unintended target. When a bomb detonates and injures someone in the distance who wasn't supposed to be affected, that's an example of collateral damage. When Hezekiah's pride resulted in the captivity of his people and his family, that too was collateral damage.

> *Be not deceived; God is not mocked: for whatsoever a man soweth, that shall he also reap. For he that soweth to his flesh shall of the flesh reap corruption; but he that soweth to the Spirit shall of the Spirit reap life everlasting.*
> —EPHESIANS 6:7–8

One of the biggest lies you can believe is that the decisions you make only affect you. A single choice can alter the course of untold people who are around you and who come after you. Remember the ship captains from the beginning of this chapter? I doubt either one of them woke up that morning hoping to be responsible for four hundred people's deaths. But one unwise choice changed history for those people and all their families and friends.

> One of the biggest lies you can believe is that the decisions you make only affect you.

Don't go through life with the mindset of "I'm just going to do whatever I want. I'm going to do what's best for me first." There's no wisdom in that, and you'll end up hurting those around you. Where there is no wisdom, there will always be collateral damage.

What a hard lesson for Hezekiah to learn, coming just after an incredible miracle in his life! He could have responded like some of us would've, by telling God how unfair this punishment was. But instead, he accepted the consequences with the attitude of humility he should've had in the first place:

> *Then said Hezekiah unto Isaiah, Good is the word of the Lord which thou hast spoken. And he said, Is it not good, if peace and truth be in my days?*—2 KINGS 20:19

He told Isaiah, "You know what? You're right. I messed up. This wasn't about me; it was about God." He repented of his pride. In fact, in a parallel accounting of this incident we read,

> *But Hezekiah rendered not again according to the benefit done unto him; for his heart was lifted up: therefore there was wrath upon him, and upon Judah and Jerusalem. Notwithstanding Hezekiah humbled himself for the pride of his heart, both he and the inhabitants of Jerusalem, so that the wrath of the Lord came not upon them in the days of Hezekiah.*—2 CHRONICLES 32:25–26

From all accounts, Hezekiah lived out the rest of his years as a faithful man who gave honor to God for all He'd done for him. And we know that not too long after this, God brought his dark horse victory by delivering Judah from Assyria and Sennacherib and blessed the nation greatly for the rest of Hezekiah's reign.

> Where there is no wisdom, there will always be collateral damage.

So what do we take from this? We need to use whatever time we have on this earth to serve God and to do His will. We need to remember that whatever we achieve in our lives is not due to our own awesomeness but the greatness of God. Rather than take credit for His accomplishments, we need to exclaim His goodness. This is the way to humility. This is the heart of a dark horse.

+ +

CONCLUSION

+ +

In late 2008 and 2009, the NBA's scouting and draft reports included statistics and evaluative comments on a twenty-one-year-old point guard from Charlotte, North Carolina, that cast doubt on his future as a league player. One report deemed him too small with substandard athleticism. Another concluded, "He's not a great finisher around the basket...he needs to considerably improve his ball handling. He will have limited success at the next level. Do not rely on him to run your team."[1] From these reports, it's clear that, despite his famous father, not many people expected Stephen Curry to make it very far in the NBA. Just a few years later,

Curry went on to surprise everyone when he led the Golden State Warriors to the 2015 NBA Championships and was awarded MVP of the league.

His talent on the court is undeniable, but what attracts fans to Curry is that, unlike many other skilled athletes, Curry doesn't brag about or take credit for his accomplishments. After making a shot he's often seen pointing his index finger skyward, and he's not shy about explaining the reason behind it. "I know why I play the game, and it's not to score thirty points a night. It's to use the stage I'm on. I've been put here for a specific purpose: to be a witness and to share my testimony as I go through it." His father added, "He understands that everything is given by the Lord and that it can be taken away, too."[2]

Hezekiah also surprised everyone with his victories in life. He also had a pretty famous dad (in a bad way), so no one expected him to have the success he did. He was young and his nation was small, but as he was faithful and careful to give God the credit, God was able to use him in a great way for a specific purpose: to deliver His people and declare His power and glory to the surrounding nations.

You may not have the most money, the most friends, the best personality, or the best upbringing—but God can still use you in a great way.

But ye are a chosen generation, a royal priesthood, an holy nation, a peculiar people; that ye should shew forth the praises of him who hath called you out of darkness into his marvellous light;—1 PETER 2:9

Most professional athletes use two different pairs of shoes. One pair is only for practicing, and the other pair is only for games. They wouldn't think of wearing their game shoes for anything else—they set them aside for a specific purpose.

In 1 Peter 2:9, God is saying the same thing to us. He created us, chose us, and set us aside for a specific purpose. That makes us extraordinary. But are you living as if you were created to be extraordinary? Or are you living for yourself and what you want, which will only ever amount to a life of mediocrity?

For I know the thoughts that I think toward you, saith the Lord, thoughts of peace, and not of evil, to give you an expected end.—JEREMIAH 29:11

God has big, exciting plans for you. Just like He did with Hezekiah, He's chosen you too for something great. You may have already experienced more than your share of difficulties and challenges, and there will probably be more ahead. But remember these lessons from Hezekiah's life:

- Take every opportunity to overcome your obstacles.
- Don't let fear eliminate your fight.

- Don't let the enemy shake your confidence.
- Draw strength from God's Word and His promises in times of struggle.
- Trust that God knows exactly what He's doing and that He's working behind the scenes on your behalf.
- Be humble; give credit for your successes to the One who made them possible.

With these lessons in mind and an awesome God with a plan paving the way ahead of you, you too will see some amazing dark horse victories in your life. So don't settle for mediocrity when you could be extraordinary. Go surprise the world. Take it by storm for God's glory and be the victor He created you to be.

NOTES

Chapter One

1. Cornell University Library (2015). *The Lincoln Presidency: Last Full Measure of Devotion.* http://rmc.library.cornell.edu/lincoln/exhibition/candidate/

2. Matthew J. Seelinger (2015). *Nightmare at the Chosin Reservoir.* Arlington, VA: The Army Historical Foundation. https://armyhistory.org/nightmare-at-the-chosin-reservoir/

3. History.com (2016). This day in history: U.S. hockey team makes miracle on ice. http://www.history.com/this-day-in-history/u-s-hockey-team-makes-miracle-on-ice

4. Pew Research Center (2015). America's Changing Religious Landscape. http://www.pewforum.org/files/2015/05/RLS-08-26-full-report.pdf

5. Catherine Rampell (Oct. 28, 2015). "What's the Scariest Thing in America? Government Corruption." *The Washington Post.* https://www.washingtonpost.com/news/rampage/wp/2015/10/28/whats-the-scariest-thing-in-america-government-corruption/

6. Anthony Lyle (2014). *Revised Chronology of the Bible.* Bloomington, IN: AuthorHouse LLC.

7. Robert Jamieson, A. R. Fausset, & David Brown (2011). *Jamieson, Fausset, and Brown's Commentary on the Whole Bible* (2nd ed.). OSNOVA. Kindle edition.

8. Arnold Dallimore (1985). *Spurgeon: A New Biography.* London: Banner of Truth Publishing.

9. Kenneth T. Walsh (Feb. 12, 2009). "The First 100 Days: Franklin Roosevelt Pioneered the 100-Day Concept." *U.S. News & World Report.* http://www.usnews.com/news/history/articles/2009/02/12/the-first-100-days-franklin-roosevelt-pioneered-the-100-day-concept

Chapter Two

1. World Wide Web Foundry (2016). "Black Bart: California's Infamous Stage Robber." http://www.blackbart.com/index.php

2. Merriam Webster Online (2016). "Compromise." http://www.merriam-webster.com/dictionary/compromise

3. Cecilia Rasmussen (April 14, 1997). "The Violent Life of Boxer Kid McCoy." *The Los Angeles Times.* http://articles.latimes.com/1997–04–14/local/me-48617_1_kid-mccoy

4. James Donald. (2012). *Chambers Etymological Dictionary of the English Language.* Arkose Press. Kindle edition.

5. Drew Hansen (August 27, 2013). "Mahalia Jackson, and King's Improvisation." *The New York Times.* http://www.nytimes.com/2013/08/28/opinion/mahalia-jackson-and-kings-rhetorical-improvisation.html?_r=0

6.   Charles Swindoll (1978). *Hand Me Another Brick*. Nashville, TN: Thomas Nelson.

Chapter Three

1.   Ryan Canner O'Mealy (2012). "18 Under 18: Austin Gutwein." ESPN. http://espn.go.com/high-school/boys-basketball/story/_/id/7622917/austin-gutwein

2.   Ministry 127. (2016). "Trust and Obey God." http://ministry127.com/resources/illustration/trust-and-obey-god

3.   Lord Byron (1824). "On This Day I Complete My Thirty-sixth Year." http://www.bartleby.com/333/621.html

Chapter Four

1.   Vivian Giang (January 1, 2014). "15 Billionaires Who Were Once Dirt Poor." *Business Insider*. http://www.businessinsider.com/billionaires-who-came-from-nothing-2013-12?op=1

2.   F. Sanello (1998). *Stallone—A Rocky Life*. Edingurgh, Scotland: Mainstream Publishing.

3.   Steve Almasy, Josh Levs, & Saeed Ahmed (April 21, 2014). "Teen hitches ride to Hawaii in jet's landing gear—and lives to tell the tale." CNN.com. http://www.cnn.com/2014/04/21/us/hawaii-plane-stowaway/

4.   Poch de la Rosa (August 7, 2015). "Arian Foster on Being Atheist: 'Faith Isn't Enough for Me." I4U News. http://www.i4u.com/2015/08/93937/arian-foster-being-atheist-faith-isnt-enough-me

5.   Reader's Digest Online (2015). "The World's Most Outrageously Expensive Vacations." http://www.rd.com/advice/travel/the-worlds-most-outrageously-expensive-vacations/

6.   UNC School of Medicine. "The Grayson Clamp Story" (2015). UNC Otolayngology/Head and Neck Surgery. https://www.med.unc.edu/ent/grayson-clamp-family-story

Chapter Five

1.   Mike Flacy (December 3, 2012). "Teenager brags about bank robbery on YouTube before getting arrested." Digital Trends.com. http://www.digitaltrends.com/web/teenager-shows-off-bank-robbery-money-on-youtube-before-arrest/
2.   Ministry 127. (2016). "The Fruit of the Bible." Reprinted from Charles Spurgeon (1870), *Feathers for Arrows.* http://ministry127.com/resources/illustration/the-fruit-of-the-bible
3.   *Christianity Today.* (July 1, 2003). "Noted Surgeon and Author Paul Brand Dies at Age 89." http://www.christianitytoday.com/ct/2003/julyweb-only/7–7-41.0.html
4.   Merriam-Webster Online Dictionary (2016). "Zeal." http://www.merriam-webster.com/dictionary/zeal

Chapter Six

1.   James F. Clarity, Milt Freudenheim, & Richard Levine (September 7, 1986). "Two Soviet Ships Collide in the Night." *The New York Times.* http://www.nytimes.com/1986/09/07/weekinreview/the-world-two-soviet-ships-collide-in-the-night.html
2.   John G. Butler (1999). *Hezekiah, the King of Survival* (Bible Biography Series). Clinton, IA: LBC Publications
3.   Butler (1999), p. 217.
4.   Reuters (August 26, 2015). "U.S. Commuters Spend About 42 Hours A Year Stuck In Traffic Jams." http://www.newsweek.com/us-commuters-spend-about-42-hours-year-stuck-traffic-jams-365970

5. Kelly Wallace (November 3, 2015). "Teens spend a 'mind-boggling' 9 hours a day using media, report says." *CNN.com*. http://www.cnn.com/2015/11/03/health/teens-tweens-media-screen-use-report/
6. Victor Luckerson (January 19, 2016). "This Is How Much Netflix We're All Watching Every Day." *Time Magazine Online*. http://time.com/4186137/netflix-hours-per-day/

Conclusion

1. Fox Sports.com (September 22, 2015). "Curry gets last laugh on haters, reads critical 2009 scouting report." http://www.foxsports.com/nba/story/steph-curry-golden-state-warriors-reads-draft-2009-scouting-report-092215
2. Charles Chandler. (March 1, 2016). "Stephen Curry: 'I Can Do All Things Through Christ." BillyGraham.org. http://billygraham.org/story/stephen-curry-i-can-do-all-things-through-christ/

ABOUT THE AUTHOR

Matt Chappell has served for the past five years as the youth pastor at Coastline Baptist Church in Oceanside, California. He and his wife, Katie, are venturing into new, exciting territory as they plant Rock Hill Baptist Church in Fontana, California.

Matt and Katie have a heart to reach Southern California and beyond with the life-giving and life-changing message of Jesus. They are excited to see how the Lord will work in this growing area of San Bernardino County.

Matt and Katie have two children, Liv and Luke. They look forward to continuing to invest their lives in the next generation.

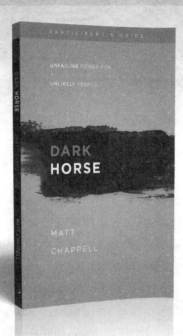

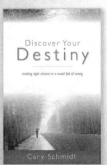

Visit us online

strivingtogether.com

wcbc.edu